CYBERSECURITY SALES MASTERY

A Comprehensive Guide for MSPs

First Edition: By Adam Anderson and Brad Powell

CONTENTS

Cybersecurity Sales Mastery

About the Authors

  Adam Anderson

  Brad Powell

Why must ThreatCaptain write this Book?

Selling Cybersecurity is Different

How to Use This Book as an MSP

Understanding the Format of This Book

Chapter 1: Introduction: Navigating the Cybersecurity Market

Chapter 2: Understanding the Cybersecurity Landscape

Chapter 3: The Art of Selling Cybersecurity

Chapter 4: Crafting Compelling Sales Pitches

Chapter 5: Building Trust and Transparency

Chapter 6: Overcoming Objections

Chapter 7: The Importance of Financial Impact Analysis

Chapter 8: Leveraging Success Stories

Chapter 9: Good vs. Great: What Sets Top MSPs Apart

Chapter 10: Collaborative Selling with Technical Teams

Chapter 11: Integrating Cybersecurity into MSP Quarterly Business Reviews (QBRs)

Chapter 12: Final Thoughts and Next Steps

Bonus Chapter: Top 7 Things an MSP Must Know to Build an Effective Cybersecurity Selling Program

Bonus Chapter: ThreatCaptain - Comprehensive SaaS Solution for

MSPs

Bonus Chapter: Using Financial Impact Simulations to Enhance Cybersecurity Sales

ABOUT THE AUTHORS

Adam Anderson

Adam Anderson is a multifaceted professional with a diverse and extensive career that spans over 20 years in cybersecurity, digital transformation, and entrepreneurship. His journey has taken him from server rooms to boardrooms and classrooms, positioning him as a thought leader, speaker, author, and change agent.

Adam's entrepreneurial spirit led him to found several ventures, including a notable cybersecurity company that he successfully sold in 2018. He is currently the Chairman of the Board for Hook Security, a behavioral science cybersecurity startup, where he focuses on integrating business strategy with cybersecurity and enhancing leadership awareness of cyber threats.

In 2019, Adam and his wife Kerry Anderson founded Ansuz Group, an initiative aimed at helping countries and governments transform through digital economy adoption. This initiative was inspired by his interactions with prominent global figures during a week-long stay on Necker Island.

Adam's expertise lies in getting things started and revitalizing failing projects or companies through creativity, humor, and servant leadership. His philosophy is that business is the paintbrush used to create the future, a heavy responsibility he embraces with joy and dedication. He strives to set an example for his children, Eva and Kenton, by working with people who aim to do amazing things and having fun along the way.

Adam's work in the British Virgin Islands fosters entrepreneurship, business governance, and digital transformation, aiming to break the economic restrictions of a tourism-based economy. His contributions to cybersecurity and digital transformation are widely recognized, and he has been featured in numerous publications and podcasts, sharing his insights on business innovation and cybersecurity.

Adam holds several professional titles and has authored multiple books on cybersecurity and business transformation. His published works include titles like "Digital Leadership: Navigating Cybersecurity in the Boardroom" and "The CMMC Blueprint: A Guide for Small and Mid-Sized Manufacturers."

Adam Anderson's extensive experience and visionary approach make him a pivotal figure in the realms of cybersecurity and digital transformation.

Brad Powell

Brad Powell is a seasoned sales entrepreneur with over 17 years of experience in cybersecurity, physical security, and SaaS technology. As a co-founder of ThreatCaptain and Hook Security, Brad has a proven track record of successful business development, partnership building, and subscription revenue growth.

At ThreatCaptain, Brad led the company from concept to ramping up business operations and revenue growth. He secured over 500 net new customers and grew the company's annual recurring revenue (ARR) to $1.5 million before handing over to professional management. His role at ThreatCaptain demonstrates his ability to lead startups to significant milestones and build sustainable revenue streams.

Prior to ThreatCaptain, Brad co-founded Hook Security, where he specialized in achieving the first $1 million ARR, mastering cold calling, and executing customer-centric sales strategies. His skills in agile business development, networking, and challenger sales have made him a sought-after speaker and podcast guest.

Brad holds a Master of Business Administration in

Entrepreneurship from The Citadel: The Military College of South Carolina, and he has studied International Business at Victoria University in Wellington, New Zealand. His educational background and practical experience have equipped him with a deep understanding of business operations and sales strategies.

In addition to his entrepreneurial ventures, Brad serves on the CompTIA Cyber Task Force board, where he contributes his expertise in cybersecurity to broader industry initiatives. His commitment to psychological security and innovative sales development has helped numerous MSPs adopt comprehensive security stacks and expand their client bases.

Brad Powell's entrepreneurial spirit, sales acumen, and dedication to cybersecurity make him a key player in the industry, continuously driving growth and innovation in the companies he leads.

Together, Adam Anderson and Brad Powell bring a wealth of knowledge, experience, and vision to the cybersecurity landscape. Their combined expertise in business development, cybersecurity, and digital transformation positions them as leaders and innovators, dedicated to helping MSPs succeed in an increasingly complex and challenging market.

WHY MUST THREATCAPTAIN WRITE THIS BOOK?

Welcome aboard, MSPs! As we embark on this journey together, let's talk about why this book exists and why it's so important for your voyage through the cybersecurity sales landscape.

Navigating the Uncharted Waters of Sales Skills

Many of you are seasoned pros when it comes to technical expertise—navigating the intricate currents of IT and cybersecurity. But when it comes to selling these crucial services, it can sometimes feel like you're adrift without a compass. The truth is, selling cybersecurity isn't about adopting a slick, used car salesperson approach. Instead, it's more akin to a doctor's visit: diagnosing problems, prescribing solutions, and caring for your clients' digital well-being.

Sales is a professional skillset, much like cybersecurity itself. It requires strategy, finesse, and a bit of charm. Just like steering a ship, mastering sales takes practice, knowledge, and the right tools to chart a successful course. Yet, many technical sellers don't realize that these skills need to be developed. Fear not! This book is here to provide you with strategies and tactics to help you build lasting relationships with your clients.

The Doctor's Visit, Not the Used Car Lot

Think about a visit to the doctor. The doctor doesn't try to sell you the latest and greatest cure-all without first understanding your symptoms. Instead, they diagnose your condition, explain your options, and recommend the best treatment plan. That's exactly how you should approach cybersecurity sales. You're not just pushing products; you're safeguarding your clients' digital health.

This approach builds trust and positions you as a trusted advisor rather than just another vendor. Clients are more likely to stay with you for the long haul when they see you have their best interests at heart. Selling cybersecurity is about understanding the client's needs, educating them on the threats they face, and guiding them to the best solutions—like a skilled navigator steering a ship through choppy waters.

Encouragement for the Reluctant Sales Mariners

Now, let's address the elephant in the room: many of you might feel out of your depth when it comes to sales. And that's perfectly normal! Most MSP salespeople aren't expected to come fully equipped with sales skills because this type of engagement is a different beast altogether. It's okay to need a bit of guidance.

After six years of navigating the treacherous waters of cybersecurity sales through the channel, we—your trusty authors —understand the unique challenges you face. As MSPs, you often have to be the "Jack of All Trades" IT service providers, juggling everything from network management to cybersecurity threats. This book is here to offer straightforward, actionable help to boost your confidence and effectiveness in selling cybersecurity.

Setting Sail with Confidence

So, why write this book? Because we believe that with the right knowledge and tools, every MSP can become proficient in cybersecurity sales. We want to equip you with the skills to not only survive but thrive in these waters. By the time you've finished this book, you'll be ready to chart your course, guide your clients safely, and achieve lasting success in cybersecurity sales.

ADAMANDERSON

Welcome aboard, and let's set sail toward success together!

SELLING CYBERSECURITY IS DIFFERENT

Selling cybersecurity solutions is fundamentally different from selling other Managed Service Provider (MSP) products and services. While traditional IT services focus on operational efficiency, uptime, and cost savings, cybersecurity deals with the invisible and ever-evolving threat landscape that poses significant risks to an organization's survival. This chapter will delve into the unique challenges and opportunities of selling cybersecurity, highlighting why a different approach is necessary and how MSPs can effectively address these differences.

The Nature of Cyber Threats

Cybersecurity threats are complex, constantly evolving, and often invisible until it's too late. Unlike other IT services that are more predictable and stable, cybersecurity requires a proactive and dynamic approach.

Constant Evolution: Cyber threats are continually changing, with new vulnerabilities and attack vectors emerging regularly. This requires continuous learning and adaptation from both MSPs and their clients.

Invisibility of Threats: Many cyber threats, such as malware and phishing attacks, can go undetected for long periods. This invisibility makes it challenging to convince clients of the urgency and necessity of robust cybersecurity measures.

Severity of Consequences: The consequences of a cyber attack can be catastrophic, including financial loss, reputational damage, and legal implications. These high stakes necessitate a different sales approach, emphasizing risk management and prevention.

The Psychological Barrier: Selling cybersecurity involves overcoming significant psychological barriers. Clients may suffer from the "it won't happen to us" mentality, making it difficult to convey the real risks they face.

Risk Perception: Many clients underestimate the likelihood and impact of cyber threats, believing they are not targets. Educating clients about the reality and prevalence of cyber attacks is crucial.

Intangible Benefits: Unlike other IT services that have clear, tangible benefits (e.g., faster processing speeds, reduced downtime), cybersecurity's benefits are often intangible until a breach occurs. This makes it harder to justify the investment.

Fear and Uncertainty: The fear of potential breaches can paralyze decision-making. MSPs need to address this fear with clear, actionable plans and reassurances that their solutions can mitigate these risks.

The Complexity of Cybersecurity Solutions

Cybersecurity solutions are inherently complex and multifaceted, involving a mix of technology, processes, and human factors. This complexity requires a more consultative and educational sales approach.

Technical Complexity: Cybersecurity technologies can be difficult to understand for non-technical stakeholders. MSPs need to simplify these concepts and focus on the benefits and outcomes rather than the technical details.

Process Integration: Effective cybersecurity involves integrating various processes, such as risk management, compliance, and incident response. MSPs must demonstrate how their solutions fit into the client's existing workflows and enhance their overall security posture.

Human Element: Many cyber threats exploit human vulnerabilities through social engineering attacks. Selling cybersecurity must include educating and training the client's workforce to recognize and respond to these threats.

The Need for Trust and Transparency

Building trust is essential in selling cybersecurity. Clients are entrusting MSPs with the protection of their most valuable assets, requiring a high degree of transparency and integrity.

Trust Building: MSPs must position themselves as trusted advisors rather than just vendors. This involves open communication, honesty about the limitations of cybersecurity measures, and a commitment to ongoing support.

Transparency: Providing clear, transparent reporting on cybersecurity measures and their effectiveness helps build trust. Clients need to see tangible proof that their investments are paying off in terms of enhanced security.

Long-Term Relationships: Cybersecurity is not a one-time purchase but an ongoing commitment. MSPs need to build long-term relationships with clients, continuously updating and improving their security posture.

Demonstrating ROI and Financial Impact: One of the biggest challenges in selling cybersecurity is demonstrating the return on investment (ROI). Clients need to see how their investment in cybersecurity translates into financial benefits.

Financial Impact Analysis: Conducting financial impact analyses helps clients understand the potential costs of a breach versus the investment in preventive measures. Tools like ThreatCaptain can quantify these risks and provide clear financial justifications for cybersecurity investments.

Case Studies and Testimonials: Sharing success stories and testimonials from other clients can help demonstrate the real-world benefits of cybersecurity solutions. Highlighting instances where significant breaches were prevented or mitigated can make a compelling case.

Ongoing Value: Emphasize the ongoing value of cybersecurity investments, such as compliance with regulations, improved customer trust, and protection of intellectual property. These benefits, though intangible, are crucial for the long-term success and sustainability of the client's business.

Selling cybersecurity is fundamentally different from selling other MSP products and services due to the unique nature of cyber threats, the psychological barriers, the complexity of solutions, the need for trust, and the challenge of demonstrating ROI. By adopting a consultative approach, focusing on education and transparency, and leveraging tools like ThreatCaptain for financial impact analysis, MSPs can effectively address these differences and build stronger, more secure client relationships.

HOW TO USE THIS BOOK AS AN MSP

Congratulations on investing in your growth as a Managed Service Provider (MSP) by exploring the intricacies of selling cybersecurity solutions. This book is designed to be a comprehensive guide, offering insights, strategies, and practical advice to help you excel in the competitive cybersecurity market. In this chapter, we'll discuss how to effectively use this book to enhance your sales efforts, build stronger client relationships, and achieve lasting success.

Start with a Self-Assessment

Before diving into the strategies and techniques presented in this book, take some time to assess your current cybersecurity sales approach. Identify your strengths and areas for improvement. This self-assessment will help you focus on the chapters and sections that are most relevant to your needs.

Key Actions:

- **Evaluate Your Sales Process:** Review your current sales process and identify any gaps or weaknesses.
- **Assess Client Relationships:** Consider the quality of your relationships with existing clients and how you can improve them.
- **Identify Knowledge Gaps:** Determine if there are specific areas where you or your team need additional knowledge or training.

Example: "After evaluating our sales process, we realized that we needed to improve our financial impact analysis skills to better demonstrate the ROI of our cybersecurity solutions. This book provided us with the tools and techniques to enhance this aspect of our sales approach."

Create a Customized Action Plan

Use the insights and strategies from this book to develop a customized action plan that addresses your specific needs and goals. This plan should outline the steps you will take to implement the best practices and techniques discussed in the book.

Key Actions:

- **Set Clear Objectives:** Define specific, measurable goals for improving your cybersecurity sales efforts.
- **Develop a Timeline:** Create a timeline for implementing the strategies and techniques outlined in the book.
- **Assign Responsibilities:** Determine who on your team will be responsible for each aspect of the action plan.

Example: "Our action plan included setting a goal to increase our client base by 20% over the next year. We developed a timeline for enhancing our sales pitches, conducting regular security assessments, and leveraging success stories to build credibility."

Integrate Best Practices into Your Sales Process

Incorporate the best practices and strategies from this book into your existing sales process. This might involve revising your sales scripts, updating your marketing materials, or enhancing your client engagement strategies.

Key Actions:

- **Revise Sales Scripts:** Update your sales scripts to include key points from the book, such as addressing common objections and demonstrating financial impact.
- **Update Marketing Materials:** Ensure that your marketing materials reflect the insights and best practices discussed in

the book.

- **Enhance Client Engagement:** Implement strategies for building trust and transparency, such as regular updates and proactive communication.

Example: "We revised our sales scripts to incorporate a more consultative approach, asking detailed questions to understand our clients' specific challenges and tailoring our solutions accordingly. This change led to more meaningful conversations and increased client trust."

Train Your Team

Ensure that your entire team is aligned with the strategies and techniques outlined in this book. Provide training sessions to help your team members understand and implement the best practices discussed.

Key Actions:

- **Conduct Training Sessions:** Hold regular training sessions to review key concepts and strategies from the book.
- **Provide Resources:** Share relevant chapters and sections of the book with your team and encourage them to read and discuss the content.
- **Encourage Feedback:** Solicit feedback from your team on how the strategies are working and what improvements can be made.

Example: "We held weekly training sessions where we reviewed different chapters of the book and discussed how to apply the strategies in our daily sales efforts. This collaborative approach helped our team feel more confident and empowered."

Measure and Adjust

Regularly measure the effectiveness of the strategies you've implemented and make adjustments as needed. Use key performance indicators (KPIs) to track your progress and identify areas for further improvement.

Key Actions:

- **Track KPIs:** Monitor key metrics such as client acquisition, retention rates, and revenue growth.
- **Review and Adjust:** Periodically review your action plan and make adjustments based on your progress and feedback from your team.
- **Celebrate Successes:** Recognize and celebrate the successes and milestones you achieve along the way.

Example: "We tracked our progress by monitoring client acquisition and retention rates. After six months, we reviewed our action plan and made adjustments to our client engagement strategies based on the feedback we received. Celebrating our successes motivated our team to continue striving for excellence."

Leverage Success Stories

As you implement the strategies from this book and achieve positive results, leverage your own success stories to build credibility and attract new clients. Document your successes and use them in your marketing and sales efforts.

Key Actions:

- **Document Successes:** Keep detailed records of your successful projects and client outcomes.
- **Create Case Studies:** Develop case studies that highlight the challenges, solutions, and results of your work.
- **Share Testimonials:** Collect and share testimonials from satisfied clients to build trust with potential clients.

Example: "We created detailed case studies of our successful projects and shared them on our website and in sales presentations. These success stories helped us demonstrate our expertise and attract new clients."

Stay Committed to Continuous Improvement

The cybersecurity landscape is constantly evolving, and so should your approach. Stay committed to continuous improvement by regularly revisiting the strategies in this book and staying informed about new developments in the field.

Key Actions:

- **Ongoing Learning:** Continue to educate yourself and your team about the latest cybersecurity trends and best practices.
- **Regular Reviews:** Periodically review the strategies and techniques in this book to ensure they remain relevant and effective.
- **Adapt and Innovate:** Be open to adapting your approach and incorporating new ideas and technologies.

Example: "We made a commitment to ongoing learning by attending industry conferences and participating in professional forums. Regularly reviewing the strategies in this book ensured that we stayed ahead of emerging threats and continued to provide the best possible service to our clients."

This book is a valuable resource designed to help you excel in the cybersecurity market. By starting with a self-assessment, creating a customized action plan, integrating best practices, training your team, measuring and adjusting your progress, leveraging success stories, and staying committed to continuous improvement, you can build an effective cybersecurity selling program that protects your clients and grows your business.

UNDERSTANDING THE FORMAT OF THIS BOOK

Our goal is to ensure that you, as an MSP, can quickly access the information you need, understand it, and apply it to enhance your cybersecurity sales efforts. This book combines narratives, real-world examples, and actionable knowledge to provide a comprehensive yet concise resource.

The Power of Narrative

Each chapter begins with a narrative that sets the stage and provides context for the topic being discussed. This approach helps you relate to the material on a deeper level and understand how it applies to your real-world experiences.

Why It Works:

- **Engagement:** Stories are naturally engaging and help maintain your interest.
- **Relatability:** Narratives make complex concepts more relatable by framing them within familiar scenarios.
- **Memory:** Stories are easier to remember than isolated facts, helping you retain the information longer.

Example: "Imagine the digital world as a vast, uncharted ocean. It's filled with opportunities for exploration and treasure but also teeming with unseen dangers lurking beneath the surface. As an MSP, you are the captain, the protector, and the trusted navigator guiding businesses safely through these perilous waters."

This narrative approach provides a compelling entry point into each chapter, helping you visualize the challenges and solutions in a real-world context.

Real-World Examples

After setting the stage with a narrative, we provide real-world examples to illustrate the key concepts and strategies discussed in each chapter. These examples show how other MSPs have successfully implemented the strategies and highlight the tangible benefits they achieved.

Why It Works:

- **Proof of Concept:** Real-world examples provide concrete proof that the strategies work.
- **Inspiration:** Seeing how others have succeeded can inspire and motivate you to apply similar approaches.
- **Clarity:** Examples clarify abstract concepts by showing how they are applied in practice.

Example: "By implementing our advanced threat detection system, a financial services firm we worked with was able to prevent several attempted breaches, saving them from potential financial and reputational damage."

These examples serve as case studies that demonstrate the effectiveness of the strategies and provide you with practical insights you can apply to your own business.

Actionable Knowledge

Each chapter concludes with actionable knowledge—clear, concise, and practical steps you can take to implement the strategies discussed. These action items are designed to be quick to read and easy to understand, ensuring you can immediately apply what you've learned.

Why It Works:

- **Efficiency:** Actionable steps are quick to read and easy to understand, saving you time.

- **Practicality:** Focused on practical steps, ensuring you can immediately apply the information.
- **Clarity:** Clear and concise instructions help you know exactly what to do next.

Example: Key Actions:

- **Conduct Training Sessions:** Hold regular training sessions to review key concepts and strategies from the book.
- **Provide Resources:** Share relevant chapters and sections of the book with your team and encourage them to read and discuss the content.
- **Encourage Feedback:** Solicit feedback from your team on how the strategies are working and what improvements can be made.

These actionable steps ensure that you can quickly translate the insights from each chapter into practical actions that enhance your cybersecurity sales efforts.

Quick Reference Guides

Throughout the book, we include quick reference guides, summaries, and key takeaways to help you quickly find and review the most important information. These guides are designed to be easy to skim and provide a fast way to refresh your memory on key concepts.

Why It Works:

- **Accessibility:** Quick reference guides make it easy to find key information without reading the entire chapter.
- **Efficiency:** Summaries and key takeaways provide a quick overview of the main points.
- **Convenience:** Easy-to-skim format allows you to quickly review and reinforce your understanding.

Example: Key Takeaways from Chapter 5: Building Trust and Transparency

- **Honesty and Transparency:** Be upfront about your solutions and set realistic expectations.
- **Consistent Communication:** Provide regular updates and maintain open lines of communication.
- **Deliver on Promises:** Ensure that you follow through on commitments and exceed client expectations.

These quick reference guides and summaries are especially useful for busy MSPs who need to access information quickly and efficiently.

Conclusion

The format of this book is designed with your needs as an MSP in mind. By combining engaging narratives, real-world examples, actionable knowledge, and quick reference guides, we ensure that you can quickly access, understand, and apply the information you need to enhance your cybersecurity sales efforts.

Our goal is to provide you with a comprehensive yet concise resource that helps you navigate the complex world of cybersecurity and build a successful, rewarding career as an MSP. Thank you for investing your time in this book, and we hope that it serves as a valuable guide on your journey to excellence in cybersecurity sales.

CHAPTER 1: INTRODUCTION: NAVIGATING THE CYBERSECURITY MARKET

Welcome to the Digital Age

Picture the digital world as a rapidly expanding marketplace, filled with opportunities for growth and innovation but also rife with risks and threats. In this landscape, businesses are like merchants navigating through a bustling bazaar, seeking to protect their assets and secure their future. Cyber threats lurk at every corner, waiting to exploit vulnerabilities. Enter the Managed Service Providers (MSPs) – the advisors and protectors, equipped with the latest cybersecurity tools and strategies to safeguard businesses in this complex environment.

As an MSP, you are not just a service provider. You are a trusted advisor, a protector, and a strategist. Your clients rely on you to navigate the complex cybersecurity landscape and protect them from ever-evolving threats. This book is your guide, designed to equip you with the strategies, insights, and practical advice needed to sell cybersecurity solutions effectively. Whether you're a seasoned professional or new to the field, this guide will help you understand the intricacies of the cybersecurity market and build strong, trusting relationships with your clients.

The Importance of Cybersecurity

In today's interconnected world, cybersecurity is not just a technical issue—it's a business imperative. The stakes are incredibly high. A single cyber incident can lead to devastating financial losses, irreparable reputational damage, and legal repercussions. For many businesses, the question is not if they will be targeted, but when. Cyber threats are evolving at an alarming pace, becoming more sophisticated and harder to detect. From ransomware and phishing attacks to data breaches and insider threats, the digital marketplace is more perilous than ever.

The impact of a cyber attack extends far beyond immediate financial losses. Businesses can face prolonged operational disruptions, loss of customer trust, and significant regulatory fines. In some cases, the damage can be so severe that it threatens the very survival of the business. Given these high stakes, it's no wonder that businesses are increasingly turning to MSPs for robust cybersecurity solutions.

Your Role as an MSP

As an MSP, you play a crucial role in this digital marketplace. You are the trusted advisor to your clients, responsible for implementing and managing cybersecurity measures that protect against a myriad of threats. But your role goes beyond just providing technical solutions. You are also an educator, a strategist, and a trusted partner. Your clients look to you for guidance on how to navigate the complex and ever-changing world of cybersecurity.

This book will help you fulfill that role more effectively. It will provide you with a deep understanding of the cybersecurity landscape, equip you with the skills to craft compelling sales pitches, and teach you how to build trust and transparency with your clients. You'll learn how to overcome objections, demonstrate the financial impact of your solutions, and leverage success stories to build credibility.

What to Expect in This Book

Here's a brief overview of what you can expect to find in the chapters ahead:

1. **Understanding the Cybersecurity Landscape:** We'll explore the current state of cybersecurity, the types of threats businesses face, and the critical importance of robust cybersecurity measures.

2. **The Art of Selling Cybersecurity:** We'll dive into the different approaches to selling cybersecurity—fear-based, product-based, and consultative—and how to balance them effectively.

3. **Crafting Compelling Sales Pitches:** Learn how to tailor your sales pitches to resonate with your clients, using storytelling and real-world examples to make your case.

4. **Building Trust and Transparency:** Discover the importance of building trust with your clients through transparent communication and consistent service.

5. **Overcoming Objections:** Get strategies for addressing common objections, from cost concerns to skepticism about effectiveness, and turning them into opportunities.

6. **The Importance of Financial Impact Analysis:** Understand how to use financial impact analysis to demonstrate the ROI of cybersecurity investments and quantify the risks of cyber incidents.

7. **Leveraging Success Stories:** Learn how to collect and present client success stories through testimonials and case studies to build credibility and close deals.

8. **Good vs. Great: What Sets Top MSPs Apart:** Identify the key differences between successful and struggling MSPs, and get best practices for selling cybersecurity effectively.

9. **Final Thoughts and Next Steps:** We'll wrap up with a look at the ongoing journey of cybersecurity sales,

building long-term partnerships, and staying proactive in the face of evolving threats.

10. **Appendix: Resources and Tools:** A list of useful resources, tools, and references to help you stay informed and enhance your cybersecurity sales efforts.

Your Journey Begins

Selling cybersecurity solutions is both an art and a science. It requires a deep understanding of the digital marketplace, the ability to build trust and communicate effectively, and the skills to demonstrate the value of your solutions convincingly. As you embark on this journey, remember that you are not just selling a product—you are providing a vital service that protects businesses and enables them to thrive in the digital age.

So, get ready to navigate the complexities of the cybersecurity market. With the knowledge and strategies in this book, you'll be well-equipped to guide your clients safely through the challenges of the digital world and build a successful, rewarding career as an MSP. Let's get started.

CHAPTER 2: UNDERSTANDING THE CYBERSECURITY LANDSCAPE

The Evolving Threat Landscape

The digital marketplace is a dynamic and ever-changing environment. Just a few years ago, cyber threats were primarily the work of isolated hackers seeking personal gain or notoriety. Today, the landscape has evolved dramatically, with cybercriminals forming sophisticated organizations that operate like businesses and nation-states engaging in cyber warfare to disrupt economies and exert geopolitical influence.

The Rise of Organized Cybercrime

Gone are the days when lone hackers posed the primary threat. Today's cybercriminals are part of highly organized groups, often referred to as cyber cartels. These groups have hierarchies, funding, and strategic goals. They conduct operations with precision, leveraging advanced technologies and tactics to infiltrate systems, steal data, and demand ransoms.

For example, consider the evolution of ransomware. What started as simple malware has now become a tool for organized crime. Ransomware-as-a-Service (RaaS) has emerged, where sophisticated ransomware developers lease their software to other criminals, sharing the profits. This business model has lowered the barrier to entry for cybercrime, making it accessible to a wider range of malicious actors.

In one notable case, a major global shipping company was brought to its knees by a ransomware attack. The attack disrupted operations across multiple countries, causing millions in losses and demonstrating the far-reaching impact of organized cybercrime. This incident highlighted how interconnected and vulnerable our global supply chains have become.

The Emergence of Nation-State Actors

The stakes have escalated even further with the involvement of nation-states in cyber warfare. Countries now see cyber attacks as a strategic tool to achieve political and economic objectives. These attacks are not just about stealing information or causing disruption—they are about gaining a strategic advantage.

Nation-state actors often target critical infrastructure, including energy grids, financial institutions, healthcare systems, and supply chains. The goal is to create chaos, undermine public confidence, and weaken adversaries without engaging in traditional warfare. These sophisticated operations are often well-funded and coordinated, making them particularly dangerous.

For instance, a coordinated cyber attack on a country's power grid can lead to widespread blackouts, causing economic disruptions and public panic. In another case, hackers associated with a nation-state infiltrated a major financial institution, manipulating data to create financial instability. These attacks demonstrate the potential for cyber warfare to inflict significant harm on civilian infrastructure and economies.

The Impact on Supply Chains

The global supply chain, already under pressure from various geopolitical tensions, has become a prime target for cybercriminals and nation-state actors. Disrupting supply chains can have cascading effects, impacting everything from manufacturing to retail, healthcare, and beyond.

Consider the case of a major automotive manufacturer whose supply chain was disrupted by a cyber attack. The attackers targeted the company's suppliers, causing delays in production and significant financial losses. This incident highlighted the vulnerability of supply chains and the importance of securing not just the primary business but also its entire network of suppliers and partners.

Similarly, nation-states have targeted supply chains to weaken economic stability. By disrupting the flow of goods and services, these actors aim to create economic turmoil and erode trust in a country's ability to protect its economic interests. The interconnected nature of modern supply chains means that an attack on one component can ripple through the entire system, magnifying the impact.

The Role of MSPs in Protecting Against Evolving Threats

Managed Service Providers (MSPs) play a critical role. You are the front line of defense, tasked with protecting your clients from these sophisticated threats. Your role involves not just implementing security measures but also staying ahead of evolving threats through continuous monitoring, threat intelligence, and proactive strategies.

As an MSP, you must educate your clients about the changing nature of cyber threats and the importance of comprehensive cybersecurity strategies. This includes understanding the specific risks to their industry, the potential impact of supply chain disruptions, and the need for resilience against nation-state attacks.

One of your key responsibilities is to develop and implement robust security frameworks that can withstand sophisticated attacks. This involves integrating advanced threat detection and response systems, conducting regular security assessments, and ensuring compliance with industry regulations. Additionally, you must foster a culture of security awareness among your clients, emphasizing the importance of vigilance and preparedness.

MSP Liability During and After a Breach

MSPs face significant liability during and after a breach. When a client experiences a cyber attack, the MSP's role and actions come under intense scrutiny. Cyber insurance companies, seeking to recover losses, often look for parties to hold accountable, and MSPs can be prime targets for litigation.

Understanding Your Liability:

When a breach occurs, questions arise about whether the MSP took all necessary steps to prevent it. If it is determined that the MSP failed to implement adequate security measures, failed to properly educate the client, or neglected to follow best practices, they could be held liable for the damages. This liability can result in significant financial and reputational damage for the MSP.

The Role of Cyber Insurance:

Cyber insurance policies are designed to cover the financial losses associated with a cyber attack. However, these policies often come with subrogation clauses, which allow the insurance company to sue third parties responsible for the breach to recover their payouts. This means that if the insurance company believes the MSP was at fault, they may pursue legal action against the MSP.

Protecting Yourself as an MSP:

To protect themselves from liability, MSPs must demonstrate that they have taken all reasonable steps to secure their clients' systems and educate them about cybersecurity risks. This includes:

1. **Comprehensive Documentation:**
   - Keep detailed records of all security measures implemented, client communications, and training sessions. Documentation can provide evidence that you have fulfilled your responsibilities and followed best practices.

2. **Client Education:**
- Regularly educate your clients about the evolving threat landscape and the importance of cybersecurity measures. Ensure they understand their role in maintaining security and the potential risks of non-compliance.
- Example: "We conducted quarterly training sessions for all employees at a healthcare provider, ensuring they were aware of the latest phishing techniques and how to avoid them."

3. **Regular Security Assessments:**
- Conduct regular security assessments and vulnerability scans to identify and mitigate risks. Provide clients with reports and recommendations for improving their security posture.
- Example: "A comprehensive security assessment for a financial services firm revealed several vulnerabilities, which we addressed immediately, significantly reducing their risk of a breach."

4. **Incident Response Planning:**
- Develop and implement detailed incident response plans for your clients. These plans should outline the steps to be taken in the event of a breach and ensure a swift and effective response.
- Example: "Our incident response plan for a manufacturing client allowed us to quickly isolate and contain a malware outbreak, minimizing downtime and data loss."

5. **Compliance and Best Practices:**
- Ensure that all security measures and practices comply with relevant regulations and industry standards. Regularly update your policies to reflect the latest best

practices.

- Example: "By adhering to the latest GDPR guidelines, we helped a retail client avoid significant fines and maintain compliance."

By taking these steps, MSPs can demonstrate their commitment to cybersecurity and reduce their liability in the event of a breach. Proactively managing risks and educating clients can also strengthen client relationships and build trust, making it clear that you are a reliable and responsible partner in their cybersecurity efforts.

CHAPTER 3: THE ART OF SELLING CYBERSECURITY

Beyond Fear and Features: The Sales Spectrum

Selling cybersecurity is not just about painting a picture of doom and gloom or rattling off a list of technical features. It's an art that requires understanding your clients' unique needs, building trust, and demonstrating the tangible value your solutions bring to their business. To excel in this, you need to master three primary approaches: fear-based, product-based, and consultative selling. Each has its place, but the real magic happens when you combine elements of all three, tailored to your client's specific situation.

Fear-Based Selling: The Wake-Up Call

Fear can be a powerful motivator. When you highlight the potential consequences of inadequate cybersecurity—data breaches, financial losses, regulatory fines—it grabs attention. This approach is particularly effective for clients who may not yet recognize the severity of the threats they face.

Example: "Imagine waking up to find that your entire customer database has been stolen, and sensitive information is now in the hands of cybercriminals. The financial fallout, legal ramifications, and loss of customer trust could cripple your business. This is not a distant possibility; it's a reality that many businesses face every day."

However, fear alone can lead to hasty decisions and erode trust over time. The key is to balance the fear of what could happen with the reassurance that your solutions provide a solid defense.

Real-World Story: "We worked with a retail company that initially didn't see the need for advanced cybersecurity. After sharing stories of similar businesses that had suffered devastating breaches, they realized the potential risks. We then reassured them with a comprehensive security plan that addressed their specific vulnerabilities, leading to a successful partnership."

Product-Based Selling: Showcasing Solutions

Highlighting the features and capabilities of your cybersecurity products is essential. Clients need to understand what they're investing in and how it will protect them. However, bombarding them with technical jargon can be overwhelming. The goal is to translate these features into clear benefits that address their specific pain points.

Example: "Our advanced threat detection system uses AI to continuously monitor network traffic and identify suspicious activity in real-time. This means that threats are detected and neutralized before they can cause any harm, ensuring the continuous operation of your business."

Connecting the features of your products to real-world benefits helps clients see the tangible value of their investment.

Real-World Story: "A financial services firm we worked with was concerned about the increasing sophistication of cyber attacks. By implementing our AI-driven threat detection system, they were able to prevent several attempted breaches, saving them from potential financial and reputational damage."

Consultative Selling: Building Relationships

This is where the real magic happens. Consultative selling involves understanding your client's business, their challenges, and their goals. It's about building a relationship based on trust and offering tailored solutions that align with their needs. This approach positions you as a trusted advisor rather than just a vendor.

Example: "Let's start by understanding your current cybersecurity posture and the specific challenges your business faces. By conducting a thorough assessment, we can identify potential vulnerabilities and develop a customized security strategy that not only protects your data but also supports your business objectives."

Consultative selling is about listening more than talking, asking the right questions, and genuinely caring about the client's success.

Real-World Story: "We partnered with a healthcare provider that was struggling with outdated security measures and increasing regulatory pressures. Through a series of detailed consultations, we developed a tailored security framework that addressed their unique challenges, ensured compliance, and ultimately improved patient data protection."

Combining Approaches: The Balanced Strategy

The most effective cybersecurity sales strategy often involves a combination of fear-based, product-based, and consultative selling. The key is to adapt your approach based on the client's needs, their level of cybersecurity maturity, and the specific context of the conversation.

Example:

- Start with a **Fear-Based** approach to highlight the urgency of cybersecurity.
- Transition to **Product-Based** selling to explain how your solutions address these threats.
- Conclude with a **Consultative** approach to tailor the conversation to the client's specific needs and build a long-term relationship.

Real-World Story: "When approaching a mid-sized manufacturing company, we began by discussing the increasing threats to their industry, including recent high-profile breaches. This grabbed their attention and highlighted the urgency. We then showcased our suite of security solutions, explaining how each feature would protect their operations. Finally, we conducted a thorough assessment of their existing infrastructure and developed a customized plan that addressed their specific vulnerabilities and business goals."

The Importance of Trust and Transparency

Building trust and maintaining transparency are crucial in the sales process. Clients need to feel confident that you have their best interests at heart and that you will deliver on your promises. This involves being honest about the limitations and potential challenges of your solutions, as well as the steps you will take to ensure their effectiveness.

Example: "Our solution is designed to significantly reduce your risk of cyber attacks, but no system can guarantee 100% protection. That's why we also offer continuous monitoring and regular assessments to adapt to new threats and ensure your defenses remain strong."

Real-World Story: "We worked with an e-commerce company that was initially skeptical about the effectiveness of our solutions. By being transparent about what our system could and couldn't do, and by providing regular updates and assessments, we built a strong, trusting relationship. They appreciated our honesty and commitment, which ultimately led to a successful long-term partnership."

CHAPTER 4: CRAFTING COMPELLING SALES PITCHES

The Power of a Well-Crafted Pitch

A well-crafted sales pitch is your opportunity to connect with potential clients, understand their needs, and present your cybersecurity solutions as the ideal fit. In cybersecurity sales, where the stakes are high and the technical details can be overwhelming, the ability to tell a compelling story and articulate the value of your solutions is critical.

Know Your Audience

The first step in crafting a compelling pitch is understanding your audience. Each business is unique, with its own set of challenges, vulnerabilities, and priorities. To resonate with potential clients, you need to tailor your pitch to their specific situation.

Research and Preparation: Before meeting with a client, invest time in researching their business. Understand their industry, the typical cybersecurity threats they face, and any recent incidents that might have heightened their awareness of cybersecurity issues. Review their website, annual reports, and any available news articles to gather insights into their operations and priorities.

Example: "When preparing for a meeting with a healthcare provider, we researched recent ransomware attacks in the healthcare sector. We discovered that patient data breaches had increased by 25% over the past year, highlighting the need for robust data protection measures."

Client-Specific Insights: Use this information to tailor your pitch. Highlight specific threats relevant to their industry, and show that you understand their unique challenges. This approach demonstrates that you are not offering a one-size-fits-all solution but are instead providing tailored, strategic advice.

Real-World Story: "We met with a mid-sized manufacturing firm that had experienced a minor data breach. By referencing industry trends and recent incidents, we demonstrated our understanding of their challenges and highlighted how our solutions could address their specific vulnerabilities. This tailored approach helped us build credibility and trust."

The Power of Storytelling

Humans are wired for stories. A well-crafted narrative can make complex concepts more relatable and memorable. In cybersecurity sales, storytelling can help you illustrate the potential impact of cyber threats and the benefits of your solutions in a way that resonates with clients.

Structure Your Story: A compelling story typically has a clear beginning, middle, and end. Start by setting the scene with the client's current situation and challenges. Then, introduce the cyber threat or incident, followed by the resolution provided by your cybersecurity solutions. Conclude with the positive outcomes and benefits experienced by the client.

Example: "Imagine this scenario: Your business is running smoothly, but unbeknownst to you, cybercriminals are lurking, waiting for the perfect moment to strike. One day, an employee clicks on a seemingly innocent email, unleashing a ransomware attack that encrypts all your critical data. Operations grind to a halt, and the attackers demand a hefty ransom. Fortunately, with our advanced threat detection and response system, this attack is identified and neutralized before it can cause any damage, allowing your business to continue operating seamlessly."

Client Success Stories: Share real-world success stories of clients who faced similar challenges and how your solutions made a difference. Use quotes and data to add authenticity and impact. These stories not only illustrate the effectiveness of your solutions but also build trust and credibility.

Real-World Story: "A financial services firm we worked with was facing increasing cyber threats. By implementing our comprehensive cybersecurity solutions, they saw a 50% reduction in security incidents within six months. The firm's CTO stated, 'Partnering with [Your MSP] has transformed our cybersecurity posture. We now feel confident that our data is protected and our business is secure.'"

Addressing Common Objections

Every sales pitch will encounter objections. These are not roadblocks but opportunities to provide further reassurance and build trust. Common objections include cost concerns, skepticism about effectiveness, and resistance to change. Being prepared with data, testimonials, and clear explanations can help you address these concerns confidently.

Cost Concerns: Clients often worry about the cost of cybersecurity solutions. To address this, emphasize the potential cost savings from avoiding breaches and the ROI of investing in robust cybersecurity measures.

Example: "While the initial investment in cybersecurity might seem significant, consider the potential costs of a data breach. On average, a data breach can cost businesses $4.35 million in recovery and fines. Our solutions not only protect your business from such costly incidents but also provide long-term savings by preventing downtime and ensuring compliance."

Skepticism About Effectiveness: Some clients may be skeptical about the effectiveness of cybersecurity solutions. Provide evidence through case studies, testimonials, and industry certifications to demonstrate the reliability and success of your solutions.

Example: "Our threat detection system is certified by leading cybersecurity organizations and has been proven effective in real-world scenarios. For instance, one of our clients, a retail company, experienced a significant reduction in attempted breaches after implementing our solution. We can start with a pilot program so you can see the benefits firsthand."

Resistance to Change: Change can be challenging for businesses, especially if they have established processes and systems. Highlight the support and training you provide to ensure a smooth transition and emphasize the long-term benefits.

Example: "We understand that integrating new solutions can be daunting. That's why we offer comprehensive training and support to make the transition as smooth as possible. Our phased implementation approach ensures minimal disruption to your operations. The long-term benefits of enhanced security and compliance far outweigh the temporary inconvenience."

Bridging the Gap: Likelihood vs. Impact

One of the most common disconnects in cybersecurity sales is the difference between selling the potential impact of a breach and addressing the client's focus on the likelihood of such an event occurring. While MSPs often emphasize the catastrophic consequences of a cyber attack, clients are more motivated by how likely they believe the breach is to happen. This mismatch can lead to a significant gap in understanding and urgency.

Selling Impact: MSPs naturally focus on the impact because the potential damage from a cyber attack can be enormous. Highlighting these worst-case scenarios helps to underscore the importance of robust cybersecurity measures.

Example: "A data breach can result in millions of dollars in losses, severe reputational damage, and legal penalties. Your customer trust could be irrevocably damaged, and the long-term financial implications could threaten the very survival of your business."

Client Focus on Likelihood: However, clients often weigh the likelihood of an event occurring more heavily than its potential impact. If they believe that the chances of experiencing a cyber attack are low, they may not prioritize investment in cybersecurity, regardless of the potential consequences.

Example: "We understand that it might feel like a cyber attack is unlikely, especially if you haven't experienced one before. However, the reality is that cyber threats are increasing, and no business is immune."

Bridging the Gap: To bridge this gap, it's crucial to balance discussions of both likelihood and impact. Use data and real-world examples to illustrate that while the likelihood of an attack might seem low, the frequency and sophistication of attacks are increasing. Emphasize that the costs of not being prepared can be far greater than the investment in preventive measures.

Strategy:

- **Educate:** Provide statistics and industry reports that highlight the increasing frequency of cyber attacks and the growing number of businesses affected.
- **Personalize:** Share real-world examples of similar businesses that were targeted, emphasizing that cybercriminals often target businesses of all sizes.
- **Visualize:** Use scenarios and impact analysis to show the potential financial and operational repercussions of a breach.

Real-World Story: "We worked with a small logistics company that initially believed they were too small to be targeted by cybercriminals. We shared statistics showing that small and mid-sized businesses are frequently targeted because they often have weaker defenses. We also presented a scenario analysis that detailed the potential costs of a breach. This helped the client understand both the likelihood and impact, leading to their decision to invest in comprehensive cybersecurity measures."

Crafting a compelling sales pitch is both an art and a science. It requires a deep understanding of your audience, the ability to tell a compelling story, and the skills to address objections effectively. By balancing discussions of impact and likelihood, and by tailoring your pitch to the specific needs and concerns of your clients, you can build stronger relationships and close more deals.

CHAPTER 5: BUILDING TRUST AND TRANSPARENCY

The Foundation of Trust

In the world of cybersecurity, trust is the cornerstone of every successful client relationship. As an MSP, your clients are entrusting you with the security of their most valuable assets—their data and their reputation. Building and maintaining this trust requires more than just technical expertise; it requires a commitment to transparency, consistent communication, and delivering on your promises.

Establishing Trust from the First Interaction

Trust begins with the first interaction. Whether it's an initial consultation, a sales meeting, or a casual conversation, every touchpoint is an opportunity to build trust. Here are key strategies to establish trust early on:

Be Honest and Transparent: From the outset, be upfront about what your solutions can and cannot do. Avoid overpromising and ensure that your clients have realistic expectations about the capabilities of your cybersecurity measures.

Example: "We have an advanced threat detection system that significantly reduces the risk of breaches. However, it's important to understand that no system can guarantee 100% protection. Our approach includes continuous monitoring and regular updates to adapt to new threats."

Listen Actively: Take the time to understand your client's specific needs, concerns, and goals. Active listening shows that you value their input and are committed to finding solutions that truly address their challenges.

Real-World Story: "During our first meeting with a healthcare provider, we listened to their concerns about patient data security and regulatory compliance. By understanding their specific challenges, we were able to tailor our solutions to meet their needs, which helped establish a foundation of trust."

Provide Clear and Concise Information: Cybersecurity can be complex and technical. Providing clear, concise, and understandable information helps clients feel more comfortable and informed about their decisions.

Example: "Let me explain how our encryption technology works in simple terms: it converts your data into a code that can only be accessed with a specific key. This means that even if data is intercepted, it cannot be read without the key."

Consistent Communication

Ongoing, consistent communication is vital to maintaining trust. Clients need to feel that they are kept in the loop and that you are proactively managing their cybersecurity needs.

Regular Updates: Provide regular updates on the status of their cybersecurity measures, any new threats, and the actions you are taking to address them. This keeps clients informed and reassured that you are actively protecting their interests.

Example: "We send monthly reports detailing all security activities, including any detected threats and how they were handled. This transparency helps our clients understand the value of our services and stay informed about their security status."

Proactive Outreach: Don't wait for clients to reach out with problems. Regularly check in with them to discuss their security posture, any changes in their environment, and potential improvements.

Real-World Story: "We schedule quarterly reviews with our clients to discuss their current security status and any emerging threats. During one review, we identified a new vulnerability in their software and immediately implemented a patch, preventing a potential breach."

Open Channels of Communication: Ensure that clients know how to reach you and that you are responsive to their inquiries and concerns. Open, two-way communication fosters a sense of partnership and trust.

Example: "We provide multiple channels for communication, including phone, email, and a dedicated client portal. Our clients know they can reach us 24/7 for any urgent issues or questions."

Delivering on Promises

Nothing erodes trust faster than unfulfilled promises. It is crucial to deliver on what you promise and to exceed client expectations whenever possible.

Set Realistic Expectations: Be clear about what clients can expect from your services, including the timeline for implementation, the level of protection, and any potential limitations.

Example: "Implementing our full cybersecurity suite will take approximately three months. During this time, we will conduct a thorough assessment, deploy the necessary tools, and provide training for your staff."

Follow Through: Ensure that you follow through on your commitments. If you promise a security assessment by a certain date, make sure it is completed on time and that the results are communicated clearly to the client.

Real-World Story: "We promised a retail client that we would enhance their threat detection capabilities within 60 days. By sticking to our timeline and providing detailed progress reports, we delivered on our promise, which strengthened their trust in our services."

Go Above and Beyond: Whenever possible, exceed client expectations. Small gestures, such as additional training sessions or personalized security tips, can make a significant difference in how clients perceive your commitment to their success.

Example: "After deploying a new security solution for a financial services firm, we provided additional training sessions tailored to their staff's specific roles. This extra effort helped them feel more confident in using the new system and reinforced their trust in our dedication to their security."

The Role of Transparency

Transparency is not just about being honest; it's about being open and clear in all your communications and actions. This includes being transparent about potential risks, the effectiveness of your solutions, and any incidents that occur.

Admit Mistakes: If a mistake happens, own up to it immediately. Explain what went wrong, what steps are being taken to fix it, and how you will prevent similar issues in the future.

Example: "We experienced a brief outage during the implementation of your security update. We identified the cause, resolved the issue, and are implementing additional checks to prevent this from happening again. We apologize for any inconvenience caused."

Share Successes and Challenges: Regularly share both the successes and challenges of your cybersecurity efforts. This balanced approach helps clients see the full picture and trust that you are handling their security comprehensively.

Real-World Story: "We recently thwarted an attempted phishing attack targeting your company. While this is a success, we also identified an area where employee training could be improved. We recommend additional training sessions to enhance your team's awareness and response to phishing attempts."

Conclusion

Building trust and maintaining transparency are essential

components of a successful cybersecurity partnership. By being honest, communicative, and reliable, you can establish strong, trusting relationships with your clients. This foundation of trust not only enhances client satisfaction but also positions you as a trusted advisor in the cybersecurity landscape.

CHAPTER 6: OVERCOMING OBJECTIONS

Turning Objections into Opportunities

In any sales process, objections are inevitable. However, objections are not roadblocks; they are opportunities to provide more information, address concerns, and build trust. In the cybersecurity market, where the stakes are high and the subject matter can be complex, being prepared to handle objections effectively is crucial to closing deals and building strong client relationships.

Understanding Common Objections

The first step in overcoming objections is understanding the common concerns that clients have. These typically include cost, skepticism about effectiveness, complexity of implementation, and resistance to change. Let's explore these objections and how to address them effectively.

Cost Concerns:

Clients often worry about the cost of cybersecurity solutions. They may perceive these solutions as expensive and question whether the investment is justified.

Example: "We understand that budgeting for cybersecurity can be challenging, especially when it seems like an additional expense. However, consider the potential cost of a data breach, which on average can exceed $4 million. Investing in robust cybersecurity measures now can save you from significant financial losses in the future."

Strategy:

- **Demonstrate ROI:** Show the potential return on investment by highlighting cost savings from avoiding breaches, fines, and downtime. Use financial impact analysis to quantify these savings.
- **Offer Flexible Solutions:** Provide options that fit different budget levels, such as phased implementations or scalable solutions.

Real-World Story: "We worked with a small e-commerce business that was concerned about the cost of cybersecurity. By demonstrating the potential financial impact of a breach and offering a scalable solution that fit their budget, we were able to show them the value of investing in cybersecurity. As a result, they experienced fewer incidents and ultimately saved money."

Skepticism About Effectiveness:

Some clients may doubt the effectiveness of cybersecurity solutions, especially if they have not experienced a breach or have used ineffective solutions in the past.

Example: "I understand your skepticism. It's natural to be cautious about investing in new technology. Let me share a case study of a similar company that implemented our solutions and saw a significant reduction in security incidents."

Strategy:

- **Provide Evidence:** Use case studies, testimonials, and industry certifications to demonstrate the effectiveness of your solutions.
- **Offer a Pilot Program:** Allow clients to test your solutions on a small scale before committing to a full implementation.

Real-World Story: "A mid-sized financial services firm was skeptical about our threat detection system. We offered them a three-month pilot program to demonstrate its effectiveness. During this period, the system detected and neutralized multiple threats, which convinced them to proceed with a full implementation."

Complexity and Implementation Concerns:

Clients may worry that integrating new cybersecurity solutions will be too complex, time-consuming, or disruptive to their operations.

Example: "I understand that implementing new technology can seem daunting. Our team specializes in seamless integrations with minimal disruption to your operations. We also provide comprehensive training and support to ensure a smooth transition."

Strategy:

- **Simplify the Process:** Break down the implementation process into manageable steps and provide clear timelines.
- **Provide Support:** Offer training, documentation, and ongoing support to ensure a smooth integration and adoption.

Real-World Story: "A healthcare provider was concerned about the complexity of integrating a new data encryption system. We assured them by outlining a clear, step-by-step implementation plan and providing training sessions for their staff. The transition was smooth, and they now benefit from enhanced data security."

Resistance to Change:

Change can be difficult for any organization, especially if they have established processes and systems in place. Clients may be resistant to adopting new solutions due to fear of disruption or uncertainty about the benefits.

Example: "It's natural to be hesitant about change, especially when it involves critical systems. However, the cybersecurity landscape is constantly evolving, and staying ahead of threats requires continuous improvement. We will work closely with your team to ensure a smooth transition and minimal disruption."

Strategy:

- **Highlight Benefits:** Emphasize the long-term benefits of the new solutions, including improved security, compliance, and operational efficiency.

- **Provide Reassurance:** Offer comprehensive support and highlight your track record of successful implementations.

Real-World Story: "A logistics company was resistant to changing their outdated security protocols. We highlighted the increased risks they faced with their current setup and provided a detailed plan for upgrading their security measures with minimal disruption. By showcasing the benefits and providing reassurances, we successfully guided them through the transition."

Bridging the Gap: Likelihood vs. Impact

One of the most common disconnects in cybersecurity sales is the difference between selling the potential impact of a breach and addressing the client's focus on the likelihood of such an event occurring. While MSPs often emphasize the catastrophic consequences of a cyber attack, clients are more motivated by how likely they believe the breach is to happen. This mismatch can lead to a significant gap in understanding and urgency.

Selling Impact: MSPs naturally focus on the impact because the potential damage from a cyber attack can be enormous. Highlighting these worst-case scenarios helps to underscore the importance of robust cybersecurity measures.

Example: "A data breach can result in millions of dollars in losses, severe reputational damage, and legal penalties. Your customer trust could be irrevocably damaged, and the long-term financial implications could threaten the very survival of your business."

Client Focus on Likelihood: However, clients often weigh the likelihood of an event occurring more heavily than its potential impact. If they believe that the chances of experiencing a cyber attack are low, they may not prioritize investment in cybersecurity, regardless of the potential consequences.

Example: "We understand that it might feel like a cyber attack is unlikely, especially if you haven't experienced one before. However, the reality is that cyber threats are increasing, and no business is immune."

Bridging the Gap: To bridge this gap, it's crucial to balance discussions of both likelihood and impact. Use data and real-world examples to illustrate that while the likelihood of an attack might seem low, the frequency and sophistication of attacks are increasing. Emphasize that the costs of not being prepared can be far greater than the investment in preventive measures.

Strategy:

- **Educate:** Provide statistics and industry reports that highlight the increasing frequency of cyber attacks and the growing number of businesses affected.
- **Personalize:** Share real-world examples of similar businesses that were targeted, emphasizing that cybercriminals often target businesses of all sizes.
- **Visualize:** Use scenarios and impact analysis to show the potential financial and operational repercussions of a breach.

Real-World Story: "We worked with a small logistics company that initially believed they were too small to be targeted by cybercriminals. We shared statistics showing that small and mid-sized businesses are frequently targeted because they often have weaker defenses. We also presented a scenario analysis that detailed the potential costs of a breach. This helped the client understand both the likelihood and impact, leading to their decision to invest in comprehensive cybersecurity measures."

Turning Objections into Closing Opportunities

Once you've addressed objections, use them as stepping stones to close the sale. Each objection you overcome brings you closer to securing the client's commitment.

Example: "Now that we've addressed your concerns about cost, effectiveness, and implementation, let's discuss the next steps. We can start with a detailed assessment of your current cybersecurity posture and develop a tailored plan that fits your needs and budget."

Strategy:

- **Summarize Key Points:** Recap the main benefits of your solutions and how they address the client's specific concerns.
- **Propose Next Steps:** Clearly outline the next steps, whether it's scheduling a follow-up meeting, conducting a security assessment, or beginning the implementation process.
- **Reinforce Commitment:** Emphasize your commitment to supporting the client throughout the process and ensuring their long-term security.

Real-World Story: "After addressing all objections, we proposed a phased implementation plan to a skeptical client. By summarizing the benefits and outlining clear next steps, we secured their commitment and began a successful partnership that significantly improved their cybersecurity posture."

Overcoming objections is a crucial part of the cybersecurity sales process. By understanding common concerns, addressing them effectively, and bridging the gap between likelihood and impact, you can turn objections into opportunities to build trust and close deals. Each objection you overcome strengthens your relationship with the client and moves you closer to a successful partnership.

CHAPTER 7: THE IMPORTANCE OF FINANCIAL IMPACT ANALYSIS

Show Them the Money

In the world of cybersecurity sales, one of the most powerful tools at your disposal is financial impact analysis. This method allows you to translate the technical aspects of cybersecurity into clear, quantifiable benefits that clients can easily understand. By demonstrating the financial impact of cyber threats and the return on investment (ROI) of cybersecurity solutions, you can make a compelling case that resonates with decision-makers.

Understanding Financial Impact Analysis

Financial impact analysis involves assessing the potential financial consequences of cyber threats and comparing them to the costs of implementing cybersecurity measures. This analysis helps clients see the tangible value of investing in cybersecurity and understand how it protects their bottom line.

Key Components of Financial Impact Analysis:

1. **Risk Assessment:**
   - Identify and evaluate the specific cyber threats that the client faces.
   - Determine the likelihood and potential impact of these

threats.

2. **Cost Analysis:**
   - Calculate the potential financial losses from a cyber attack, including direct costs (e.g., ransom payments, legal fees, recovery costs) and indirect costs (e.g., reputational damage, loss of business, regulatory fines).
   - Estimate the costs of implementing cybersecurity solutions, including initial investments and ongoing maintenance.

3. **ROI Calculation:**
   - Compare the potential financial losses from a cyber attack to the costs of cybersecurity solutions.
   - Highlight the savings and benefits of investing in preventive measures.

Real-World Example: "A mid-sized manufacturing company faced significant risks from ransomware attacks. Through a detailed financial impact analysis, we demonstrated that the potential losses from a successful attack could exceed $2 million, while the cost of implementing our comprehensive cybersecurity solutions was only $250,000. This clear comparison helped the client understand the financial benefits of investing in cybersecurity."

Quantifying the Risks

To effectively use financial impact analysis, it's crucial to quantify the risks that clients face. This involves understanding the specific threats to their industry and business and translating these threats into financial terms.

Direct Costs:

- **Ransom Payments:** The cost of paying a ransom to regain access to encrypted data.
- **Recovery Costs:** Expenses related to restoring systems, recovering data, and mitigating the effects of an attack.

- **Legal Fees:** Costs associated with legal actions, regulatory fines, and compliance issues.

Indirect Costs:

- **Reputational Damage:** Loss of customer trust and potential decline in business due to negative publicity.
- **Operational Disruptions:** Downtime and productivity losses resulting from an attack.
- **Regulatory Fines:** Penalties for failing to comply with data protection regulations.

Example: "For a retail client, we calculated the potential direct costs of a data breach, including $500,000 in recovery costs, $300,000 in legal fees, and $200,000 in ransom payments. Indirect costs, such as reputational damage and lost business, were estimated to be an additional $1 million. This comprehensive assessment highlighted the severe financial impact of a breach."

Demonstrating ROI

Once you've quantified the risks, the next step is to demonstrate the ROI of cybersecurity solutions. This involves showing how the investment in cybersecurity can save clients money by preventing costly incidents and ensuring business continuity.

Example: "By investing $200,000 in our advanced threat detection and response system, a financial services firm avoided potential losses of $1.5 million from a major data breach. The ROI calculation showed that for every dollar spent on cybersecurity, the client saved $7.50 in potential losses."

Steps to Calculate ROI:

1. **Identify Savings:** Determine the potential savings from avoiding cyber incidents, including both direct and indirect costs.
2. **Calculate Costs:** Add up the total costs of implementing and maintaining cybersecurity solutions.

3. **Compare and Analyze:** Compare the savings to the costs and calculate the ROI. Use this data to highlight the financial benefits of the investment.

Real-World Story: "A healthcare provider was hesitant about the cost of our cybersecurity solutions. By conducting a financial impact analysis, we showed that their potential losses from a data breach could reach $3 million, while the cost of our solutions was only $350,000. The ROI calculation demonstrated a significant financial benefit, convincing them to proceed with the investment."

Communicating Financial Impact

Effectively communicating the financial impact of cybersecurity is crucial in making your case. Use clear, straightforward language and visual aids, such as charts and graphs, to illustrate the data. Tailor your communication to the client's level of understanding and focus on the financial benefits that matter most to them.

Example: "Here's a visual comparison of the potential costs of a cyber attack versus the investment in our cybersecurity solutions. As you can see, the savings from avoiding an attack far outweigh the costs of implementing our solutions. This investment not only protects your data but also ensures the long-term stability and success of your business."

Real-World Story: "We presented a detailed financial impact report to the board of a logistics company, using charts to show the potential losses from a ransomware attack compared to the cost of our solutions. The clear visual representation helped the board members, who were not all technical experts, understand the financial benefits. This led to unanimous approval for the cybersecurity investment."

Building a Compelling Business Case

To build a compelling business case for cybersecurity investments, combine your financial impact analysis with real-world examples, case studies, and testimonials. Show how your solutions have helped other clients avoid costly incidents and achieve a positive ROI.

Example: "Let's look at a case study of a similar business in your industry. They faced the same cyber threats and were initially hesitant about the investment. After implementing our solutions, they avoided a major data breach that would have cost them $2 million. Their actual investment was $300,000, resulting in substantial savings and a significant ROI."

Real-World Story: "A retail client was initially skeptical about the value of our cybersecurity solutions. By presenting a detailed business case that included financial impact analysis, case studies, and testimonials from other clients, we demonstrated the clear financial benefits. This comprehensive approach convinced the client to proceed with the investment, ultimately saving them from a potential breach."

Financial impact analysis is a powerful tool for demonstrating the value of cybersecurity investments. By quantifying the risks, calculating the ROI, and effectively communicating the financial benefits, you can make a compelling case that resonates with decision-makers. This approach not only helps you close deals but also builds trust and credibility with your clients.

CHAPTER 8: LEVERAGING SUCCESS STORIES

The Power of Testimonials and Case Studies

In the world of cybersecurity sales, few tools are as powerful as testimonials and case studies. These real-world examples provide concrete proof of the effectiveness of your solutions and help build credibility with potential clients. By showcasing how your cybersecurity services have successfully protected other businesses, you can create compelling narratives that resonate with decision-makers and demonstrate the tangible value you offer.

Crafting Compelling Case Studies

A good case study tells a story. It should illustrate the journey of a client from facing a significant cybersecurity challenge to achieving a successful outcome with your help. Here's how to structure a compelling case study:

1. The Client's Challenge: Begin by describing the client's business and the specific cybersecurity challenges they faced. This sets the stage and helps potential clients relate to the situation.

Example: "XYZ Corp, a mid-sized retail company, was struggling with frequent phishing attacks that compromised customer data and disrupted operations. They were concerned about the growing sophistication of these attacks and the potential financial and reputational damage."

2. The Solution: Detail the cybersecurity solutions you implemented to address the client's challenges. Explain why these solutions were chosen and how they were tailored to the client's specific needs.

Example: "To address XYZ Corp's challenges, we implemented a comprehensive cybersecurity suite, including advanced threat detection, employee training programs, and multi-factor authentication. These measures were designed to enhance their security posture and protect against sophisticated phishing attacks."

3. The Results: Highlight the positive outcomes and benefits that the client experienced as a result of your solutions. Use data and metrics to provide concrete evidence of the impact.

Example: "Within six months of implementing our solutions, XYZ Corp saw a 70% reduction in phishing attacks and a significant improvement in their overall security posture. The enhanced protection not only safeguarded customer data but also restored customer trust and boosted business continuity."

4. Client Testimonials: Include direct quotes from the client that emphasize their satisfaction with your services and the benefits they experienced. Testimonials add authenticity and personal endorsement to your case study.

Example: "John Doe, CTO of XYZ Corp, stated, 'Partnering with [Your MSP] has been a game-changer for us. Their comprehensive approach to cybersecurity has significantly reduced our risk and given us peace of mind.'"

Collecting and Using Testimonials

Testimonials from satisfied clients can be powerful tools in your sales arsenal. They provide social proof and help potential clients feel more confident in choosing your services. Here's how to effectively collect and use testimonials:

Ask for Feedback: Regularly ask your clients for feedback on your services. Positive feedback can be turned into testimonials, while constructive criticism can help you improve your offerings.

Example: "After completing a successful project with a healthcare provider, we asked them to share their experience with our services. Their positive feedback highlighted the improvements in data security and compliance."

Highlight Specific Benefits: When requesting testimonials, encourage clients to mention specific benefits they experienced. Detailed testimonials that mention concrete results are more impactful.

Example: "Thanks to [Your MSP]'s advanced threat detection system, we were able to prevent several attempted breaches and avoid potential financial losses."

Use Across Channels: Incorporate testimonials into your sales materials, website, presentations, and social media. Consistently showcasing positive client experiences reinforces your credibility.

Example: "Our website features a dedicated testimonials section, showcasing client success stories across various industries. These testimonials provide potential clients with reassurance of our expertise and the value we deliver."

Creating a Library of Success Stories

Building a library of success stories and case studies can be an invaluable resource for your sales team. These stories provide a rich source of content that can be used in sales pitches, presentations, and marketing materials.

Diverse Range of Stories: Ensure your library includes success stories from a diverse range of industries and business sizes. This demonstrates your ability to handle various challenges and tailor solutions to different needs.

Example: "Our success story library includes case studies from industries such as healthcare, retail, finance, and manufacturing, highlighting our versatility and expertise in addressing industry-specific cybersecurity challenges."

Regular Updates: Continuously update your library with new success stories and testimonials. This keeps your content fresh and relevant and shows potential clients that you are actively helping businesses like theirs.

Example: "We update our success story library quarterly, adding new case studies and testimonials to reflect our latest achievements and innovations."

Easy Access: Make your success stories easily accessible to your sales team. Provide them with templates and guidelines for incorporating these stories into their pitches and presentations.

Example: "Our sales team has access to a digital library of success stories, complete with templates and best practices for using them in client meetings and presentations. This ensures they can quickly reference relevant examples during their pitches."

Sharing Success Stories in Sales Pitches

Integrating success stories into your sales pitches can make your presentations more compelling and relatable. Here's how to effectively share success stories during sales meetings:

Tailor to the Client: Choose success stories that are relevant to the potential client's industry, size, and specific challenges. This makes the stories more relatable and impactful.

Example: "When pitching to a mid-sized financial services firm, we shared a success story of another financial client who faced similar cybersecurity challenges and achieved significant improvements with our solutions."

Use Storytelling Techniques: Present success stories in a narrative format, highlighting the client's journey from challenge to success. This makes the story more engaging and memorable.

Example: "Let me tell you about a healthcare provider we worked with. They were facing increasing regulatory pressures and frequent data breaches. By implementing our comprehensive cybersecurity solutions, they transformed their security posture and achieved full compliance within six months."

Incorporate Visuals: Use visuals such as charts, graphs, and infographics to illustrate the results of your success stories. Visual aids can make complex data more digestible and impactful.

Example: "Our presentation included a graph showing the 70% reduction in phishing attacks experienced by XYZ Corp after implementing our solutions. This visual representation reinforced the effectiveness of our services."

Leveraging success stories and testimonials is a powerful way to build credibility and attract new clients. By crafting compelling case studies, collecting detailed testimonials, and integrating these stories into your sales pitches, you can demonstrate the tangible value of your cybersecurity solutions. Success stories not only highlight your expertise but also provide potential clients with reassurance and confidence in your ability to protect their business.

CHAPTER 9: GOOD VS. GREAT: WHAT SETS TOP MSPS APART

The Difference Between Success and Struggle

Not all Managed Service Providers (MSPs) are created equal. Some excel in selling cybersecurity solutions and building lasting client relationships, while others struggle to gain traction. Understanding what sets the top performers apart can help you elevate your own sales efforts and achieve greater success.

The Key Traits of Top-Performing MSPs

1. Deep Understanding of Client Needs

Top MSPs take the time to understand their clients' unique needs, challenges, and goals. They don't offer one-size-fits-all solutions but instead provide tailored services that address specific pain points.

Example: "During our initial consultation with a manufacturing firm, we identified their primary concern was protecting intellectual property. We tailored our solutions to include advanced data encryption and access controls, specifically addressing their need to safeguard sensitive information."

2. Proactive and Consultative Approach

Successful MSPs adopt a consultative approach, positioning themselves as trusted advisors rather than just vendors. They proactively identify potential risks and opportunities for improvement, providing strategic guidance to their clients.

Example: "By conducting regular security assessments and staying ahead of emerging threats, we proactively advised a financial services client on enhancing their security posture. This consultative approach not only prevented breaches but also positioned us as a valuable partner in their business growth."

3. Strong Emphasis on Education and Training

Top MSPs prioritize client education and training. They ensure that clients understand the importance of cybersecurity and are equipped with the knowledge and skills to maintain a secure environment.

Example: "We provided comprehensive cybersecurity training for all employees of a healthcare provider, helping them recognize and respond to phishing attempts. This education significantly reduced the number of successful phishing attacks and empowered the client to maintain a vigilant security posture."

4. Effective Communication and Transparency

Clear, consistent communication and transparency are hallmarks of top-performing MSPs. They keep clients informed about the status of their cybersecurity measures, potential risks, and the steps being taken to mitigate those risks.

Example: "We maintain open lines of communication with our clients, providing regular updates through monthly reports and quarterly review meetings. This transparency builds trust and ensures that clients are always aware of their security status."

5. Demonstrated Expertise and Credibility

Top MSPs establish their expertise and credibility through certifications, industry recognition, and a proven track record of success. They leverage their reputation to build confidence and trust with potential clients.

Example: "Our certifications from leading cybersecurity organizations, combined with testimonials from satisfied clients, showcase our expertise and reliability. This credibility helps us attract new clients and reinforce our value to existing ones."

6. Commitment to Continuous Improvement

The best MSPs are committed to continuous improvement. They stay updated on the latest cybersecurity trends, technologies, and best practices, ensuring that their services remain cutting-edge and effective.

Example: "We regularly attend industry conferences and training programs to stay abreast of the latest developments in cybersecurity. This commitment to continuous learning allows us to offer innovative solutions and stay ahead of emerging threats."

7. Personalized and Scalable Solutions

Top MSPs offer personalized and scalable solutions that can grow with their clients' needs. They provide flexible options that accommodate different budgets and business sizes, ensuring that their services remain accessible and effective.

Example: "We offer scalable cybersecurity packages that allow clients to start with essential protections and gradually add more advanced features as their needs and budgets grow. This flexibility ensures that clients receive the right level of protection at every stage of their business growth."

Avoiding Common Pitfalls

1. One-Size-Fits-All Solutions

Struggling MSPs often fall into the trap of offering generic solutions that don't address the specific needs of their clients. This approach can lead to dissatisfaction and a lack of trust.

Example: "A retail client felt that their previous MSP didn't understand their unique challenges and provided generic solutions that failed to protect against targeted attacks. By offering tailored solutions that addressed their specific vulnerabilities, we were able to win their trust and business."

2. Reactive Instead of Proactive

Many MSPs only react to issues as they arise, rather than proactively identifying and addressing potential risks. This reactive approach can leave clients vulnerable and erode trust.

Example: "A logistics company was frustrated with their MSP's reactive approach to cybersecurity. By conducting regular assessments and providing proactive recommendations, we demonstrated our commitment to their security and won their business."

3. Lack of Client Education

Struggling MSPs often fail to educate their clients about the importance of cybersecurity and how to maintain a secure environment. This lack of education can lead to increased vulnerabilities and client dissatisfaction.

Example: "An e-commerce client experienced frequent security incidents due to a lack of employee training. By implementing a comprehensive training program, we helped them reduce incidents and improve their overall security posture."

4. Poor Communication

Inconsistent or unclear communication can lead to misunderstandings, dissatisfaction, and a lack of trust. Struggling MSPs often fail to keep their clients informed and engaged.

Example: "A healthcare provider switched to our services after experiencing poor communication with their previous MSP. By providing regular updates and maintaining open lines of communication, we built a strong and trusting relationship."

5. Inadequate Demonstration of Value

Many MSPs struggle to clearly demonstrate the value of their services. Without concrete examples and data, clients may not see the benefits of investing in cybersecurity.

Example: "We used detailed financial impact analysis to show a potential client the cost savings from avoiding breaches. This clear demonstration of value helped them understand the benefits of our services and led to a successful partnership."

The difference between good and great MSPs often comes

down to understanding client needs, adopting a proactive and consultative approach, emphasizing education and communication, demonstrating expertise, and committing to continuous improvement. By focusing on these key traits and avoiding common pitfalls, you can elevate your cybersecurity sales efforts and build lasting, successful client relationships.

CHAPTER 10: COLLABORATIVE SELLING WITH TECHNICAL TEAMS

Successful sales often depend on the seamless collaboration between sales professionals and technical teams. While salespeople bring in-depth knowledge of client needs and relationship-building skills, technical teams provide the expertise necessary to demonstrate the efficacy and value of cybersecurity solutions. This chapter explores the importance of collaborative selling, offers strategies for fostering effective teamwork, and highlights the benefits of integrating technical expertise into the sales process.

The Importance of Collaborative Selling

Collaborative selling in the context of cybersecurity involves leveraging the strengths of both sales and technical teams to provide a comprehensive, convincing value proposition to potential clients. This approach is particularly crucial in cybersecurity sales due to the highly technical nature of the products and services being offered.

Key Benefits:

- **Enhanced Credibility:** Technical experts can provide detailed explanations and demonstrations, enhancing the

credibility of the sales pitch.
- **Comprehensive Solutions:** Combining sales insights with technical knowledge ensures that proposed solutions are both feasible and tailored to the client's specific needs.
- **Increased Trust:** Clients are more likely to trust a team that can clearly articulate both the business and technical benefits of a solution.

Strategies for Effective Collaboration

To maximize the benefits of collaborative selling, it is essential to establish clear communication, mutual respect, and a shared vision between sales and technical teams. Here are some strategies to foster effective collaboration:

1. Establish Clear Roles and Responsibilities Define the roles and responsibilities of both sales and technical team members in the sales process. This clarity helps prevent misunderstandings and ensures that each team member knows their contribution.

Example: "Sales representatives are responsible for understanding client needs, managing relationships, and presenting business cases, while technical experts focus on providing detailed technical explanations, conducting demonstrations, and addressing technical questions."

2. Foster Open Communication Encourage open and continuous communication between teams. Regular meetings, both formal and informal, can help ensure that everyone is on the same page and can address any issues promptly.

Example: "We hold weekly alignment meetings where sales and technical teams discuss ongoing opportunities, share updates, and plan joint client engagements. This practice helps maintain transparency and coordination."

3. Conduct Joint Client Meetings Whenever possible, include both sales and technical representatives in client meetings. This approach ensures that all client questions, both business and technical, can be answered comprehensively.

Example: "During client meetings, the salesperson presents the overall value proposition, while the technical expert provides in-depth demonstrations and answers specific technical questions. This joint effort ensures a seamless and convincing presentation."

4. Develop Mutual Respect and Understanding Foster a culture of mutual respect and understanding between sales and technical teams. Recognize and value each team's unique contributions to the sales process.

Example: "We organize team-building activities and cross-training sessions to help sales and technical team members understand each other's roles and challenges. This practice builds empathy and respect, enhancing collaboration."

5. Utilize Collaborative Tools Leverage collaborative tools and platforms to facilitate communication and information sharing. Tools such as shared CRM systems, project management software, and collaboration platforms can streamline workflows and improve coordination.

Example: "We use a shared CRM system where both sales and technical teams can update client interactions, track progress, and access important documents. This centralized platform ensures that everyone has the information they need."

The Role of Technical Teams in Sales

Technical teams play a critical role in the sales process, providing the expertise needed to validate and enhance the value proposition presented by the sales team. Here are some specific ways technical teams contribute to successful cybersecurity sales:

1. Conducting Technical Demonstrations Technical experts can conduct live demonstrations of cybersecurity solutions, showing potential clients how the products work in real-world scenarios. These demonstrations help clients understand the practical benefits and effectiveness of the solutions.

Example: "A technical expert demonstrates the advanced threat detection capabilities of our cybersecurity platform, highlighting how it identifies and neutralizes potential threats in real-time."

2. Addressing Technical Questions During sales presentations and client meetings, technical team members can answer detailed technical questions, providing the depth of knowledge needed to reassure clients about the solution's capabilities.

Example: "When a client asks about the encryption standards used by our solution, the technical expert provides a detailed explanation, including the specific algorithms and protocols employed."

3. Designing Customized Solutions Technical teams can work with sales teams to design customized cybersecurity solutions that address the unique needs and challenges of each client. This tailored approach enhances the perceived value and relevance of the offering.

Example: "Based on the client's specific security requirements and existing infrastructure, our technical team designs a customized solution that integrates seamlessly with their systems and addresses their unique vulnerabilities."

4. Validating Feasibility Technical experts can validate the feasibility of proposed solutions, ensuring that what is being promised to the client can be delivered effectively and efficiently.

Example: "Before finalizing the proposal, the technical team conducts a feasibility assessment to confirm that the recommended solution can be implemented within the client's technical environment and budget constraints."

Case Study: Successful Collaborative Selling

To illustrate the power of collaborative selling, let's consider a case study involving a mid-sized financial services firm. The firm faced increasing cyber threats and needed a comprehensive cybersecurity solution.

Situation: The sales team identified the opportunity and scheduled an initial meeting with the client. Recognizing the complexity of the client's needs, the sales representative included a technical expert in the meeting.

Approach: During the meeting, the sales representative outlined the business benefits of the proposed solution, focusing on risk reduction, regulatory compliance, and cost savings. The technical expert then conducted a live demonstration of the solution's capabilities, answered detailed technical questions, and provided insights into the implementation process.

Outcome: The client was impressed by the thoroughness and expertise of the combined team. The technical demonstration and detailed answers reassured them of the solution's effectiveness and feasibility. As a result, the client decided to move forward with the proposed solution, leading to a successful sale and a long-term partnership.

Conclusion

Collaborative selling with technical teams is essential for successful cybersecurity sales. By combining the relationship-building and client-focused skills of sales professionals with the deep expertise and technical knowledge of cybersecurity experts, MSPs can provide a compelling and comprehensive value proposition. This approach not only enhances credibility and trust but also ensures that clients receive solutions that are both effective and tailored to their specific needs. By fostering open communication, mutual respect, and a collaborative culture, MSPs can maximize the strengths of both sales and technical teams, leading to greater success in the competitive cybersecurity market.

CHAPTER 11: INTEGRATING CYBERSECURITY INTO MSP QUARTERLY BUSINESS REVIEWS (QBRS)

Quarterly Business Reviews (QBRs) are essential touchpoints for Managed Service Providers (MSPs) to engage with their clients, review performance, and plan for the future. Traditionally focused on operational efficiency and cost management, QBRs present a valuable opportunity to integrate cybersecurity discussions. This chapter explores how to effectively incorporate cybersecurity into QBRs, using a fiduciary-based selling approach and leveraging tools like ThreatCaptain to address real business problems and demonstrate value.

The Importance of Cybersecurity in QBRs

Cybersecurity is a critical component of an organization's overall health and resilience. Including cybersecurity in QBRs helps clients understand their security posture, recognize emerging threats, and appreciate the value of proactive measures. It also positions the MSP as a trusted advisor who prioritizes the client's long-term success.

Key Benefits:

- **Enhanced Awareness:** Clients become more aware of the cybersecurity landscape and their own vulnerabilities.
- **Informed Decision-Making:** Regular updates enable clients to make informed decisions about their security investments.
- **Proactive Risk Management:** Addressing cybersecurity in QBRs helps identify and mitigate risks before they become serious issues.

Structuring Cybersecurity Discussions in QBRs

To effectively integrate cybersecurity into QBRs, it's important to structure the discussion in a way that is clear, actionable, and relevant to the client's business objectives. Here's a framework for structuring these discussions:

1. Review of Current Security Posture

Begin by reviewing the client's current cybersecurity posture. Use data and insights from tools like ThreatCaptain to provide a clear picture of their security status.

Key Points to Cover:

- **Recent Assessments:** Present findings from recent security assessments and audits.
- **Incident Reports:** Discuss any security incidents that occurred in the past quarter and the response actions taken.
- **Threat Landscape:** Highlight emerging threats that are relevant to the client's industry and operations.

Example: "We conducted a comprehensive security assessment last month using ThreatCaptain, which revealed that while your firewall and anti-virus systems are robust, there are vulnerabilities in your email security that need addressing."

2. Financial Impact Analysis

Use financial impact simulations to quantify the potential costs of cyber threats and the value of cybersecurity investments. This helps clients see the tangible benefits of their security measures.

Key Points to Cover:

- **Cost of Potential Breaches:** Present data on the potential financial impact of various cyber threats.
- **ROI of Security Measures:** Show the return on investment for current and proposed cybersecurity measures.
- **Savings Realized:** Highlight any cost savings from avoided incidents or reduced risks.

Example: "According to ThreatCaptain's financial impact analysis, a phishing attack could potentially cost your business up to $500,000. By investing in advanced email security measures, you can mitigate this risk and save significantly in the long run."

3. Proactive Recommendations

Provide tailored recommendations for improving the client's cybersecurity posture. Focus on actionable steps that align with their business goals and risk tolerance.

Key Points to Cover:

- **Immediate Actions:** Identify any urgent security measures that need to be implemented.
- **Long-Term Strategies:** Suggest strategic initiatives for ongoing improvement, such as employee training, policy updates, and technology upgrades.
- **Compliance Requirements:** Ensure the client is aware of and compliant with relevant industry regulations and standards.

Example: "To address the vulnerabilities in your email security, we recommend implementing multi-factor authentication and conducting regular phishing simulation training for your employees."

4. Success Stories and Case Studies

Share success stories and case studies that demonstrate the effectiveness of your cybersecurity solutions. This helps build trust and confidence in your recommendations.

Key Points to Cover:

- **Similar Client Examples:** Present case studies of similar clients who have successfully mitigated risks with your solutions.
- **Quantifiable Results:** Highlight specific outcomes, such as reduced incidents, cost savings, and improved compliance.

Example: "One of our clients in the healthcare sector faced similar email security challenges. By implementing our recommended measures, they saw a 60% reduction in phishing incidents and saved over $200,000 in potential breach costs."

5. Interactive Q&A Session

Encourage an open dialogue where clients can ask questions and express concerns. This fosters a collaborative atmosphere and ensures that the discussion addresses their specific needs.

Key Points to Cover:

- **Address Concerns:** Listen to the client's concerns and provide detailed, reassuring answers.
- **Clarify Recommendations:** Ensure the client fully understands the proposed measures and their benefits.
- **Gather Feedback:** Solicit feedback on the current cybersecurity approach and any additional needs or preferences.

Example: "Do you have any questions about the recommended email security measures? We're here to ensure you fully understand the benefits and how they will be implemented."

Leveraging ThreatCaptain in QBRs

ThreatCaptain is a valuable tool for integrating cybersecurity into

QBRs. Its features provide the data and insights needed to make compelling, data-driven arguments for enhancing cybersecurity measures.

Using ThreatCaptain:

- **Real-Time Threat Intelligence:** Provide up-to-date information on the latest threats relevant to the client's industry.
- **Financial Impact Simulations:** Quantify the potential financial consequences of cyber threats and the value of preventive measures.
- **Customized Reports:** Generate detailed, client-specific reports that highlight their current security posture, risks, and recommended actions.

Example: "ThreatCaptain's latest report shows that there has been a significant increase in ransomware attacks in your industry. We recommend strengthening your backup and disaster recovery plans to mitigate this risk."

Integrating cybersecurity into Quarterly Business Reviews (QBRs) is essential for maintaining a proactive and comprehensive approach to client management. By structuring these discussions effectively and leveraging tools like ThreatCaptain, MSPs can enhance client awareness, demonstrate the value of cybersecurity investments, and build stronger, more trusting relationships. Adopting the role of a trusted advisor, MSPs can ensure that their clients are well-protected against evolving cyber threats and positioned for long-term success.

CHAPTER 12: FINAL THOUGHTS AND NEXT STEPS

The Ongoing Journey of Cybersecurity Sales

Selling cybersecurity is not a one-time event but an ongoing journey. The digital landscape is constantly evolving, and new threats emerge regularly. As an MSP, your role is to stay ahead of these threats, continuously improve your offerings, and build long-term partnerships with your clients. In this final chapter, we'll explore how to maintain momentum, deepen client relationships, and stay proactive in the ever-changing world of cybersecurity.

Building Long-Term Partnerships

The most successful MSPs understand that building long-term partnerships with clients is the key to sustained success. Here's how to cultivate and maintain these relationships:

1. Continuous Engagement and Support: Stay engaged with your clients beyond the initial sale. Provide ongoing support, regular updates, and proactive recommendations to ensure their cybersecurity measures remain effective.

Example: "We hold quarterly review meetings with our clients to discuss their current security status, any new threats, and potential improvements. This continuous engagement helps us stay aligned with their needs and build strong, lasting partnerships."

2. Personalized Service and Custom Solutions: Offer personalized service and tailor your solutions to meet the specific needs of each client. This approach demonstrates your commitment to their success and helps build trust.

Example: "We developed a custom security solution for a financial services firm, addressing their unique regulatory requirements and risk profile. By providing personalized service, we strengthened our relationship and ensured their ongoing satisfaction."

3. Demonstrating Value Over Time: Consistently demonstrate the value of your services by sharing success stories, presenting impact analyses, and highlighting cost savings. Show clients the tangible benefits they receive from their investment in cybersecurity.

Example: "We provide our clients with annual reports that highlight the threats we've mitigated, the improvements in their security posture, and the financial savings from avoiding breaches. These reports help clients see the ongoing value of our services."

Staying Proactive and Ahead of Threats

In the rapidly changing world of cybersecurity, staying proactive is essential. Here are strategies to ensure you remain ahead of emerging threats:

1. Continuous Learning and Improvement: Stay updated on the latest cybersecurity trends, technologies, and best practices. Invest in ongoing training and certifications for your team to ensure they have the skills and knowledge to tackle new challenges.

Example: "Our team regularly attends industry conferences, participates in webinars, and completes advanced certifications. This commitment to continuous learning allows us to offer cutting-edge solutions and stay ahead of emerging threats."

2. Leveraging Threat Intelligence: Utilize threat intelligence to identify and respond to new threats before they impact your clients. Implement advanced monitoring and detection systems to stay vigilant.

Example: "We use advanced threat intelligence platforms to monitor global cyber threats and identify potential risks to our clients. This proactive approach enables us to address vulnerabilities before they can be exploited."

3. Regular Security Assessments: Conduct regular security assessments and vulnerability scans for your clients. Provide actionable recommendations and work with them to implement necessary improvements.

Example: "We perform bi-annual security assessments for our clients, identifying any new vulnerabilities and providing detailed action plans to address them. This proactive strategy helps our clients maintain a strong security posture."

4. Collaborating with Clients: Work closely with your clients to develop and implement comprehensive cybersecurity strategies. Foster a collaborative relationship where clients feel comfortable sharing their concerns and feedback.

Example: "We collaborate with our clients to develop tailored cybersecurity strategies that align with their business goals and risk profile. By fostering an open and collaborative relationship, we ensure that their security measures are effective and responsive to their needs."

Adapting to Change and Innovation

The cybersecurity landscape is not static, and neither should be your approach. Embrace change and innovation to stay relevant and effective:

1. Embracing New Technologies: Stay open to adopting new technologies and tools that can enhance your cybersecurity offerings. Evaluate emerging solutions and integrate them into your service portfolio when they provide clear benefits.

Example: "We integrated a cutting-edge AI-driven threat

detection system into our service offerings, providing our clients with enhanced protection against sophisticated cyber attacks. This innovation has significantly improved our clients' security and set us apart from competitors."

2. Flexibility and Scalability: Offer flexible and scalable solutions that can adapt to the changing needs of your clients. Ensure that your services can grow with their business and accommodate new challenges.

Example: "Our scalable cybersecurity packages allow clients to start with essential protections and gradually add more advanced features as their needs and budgets grow. This flexibility ensures that our services remain relevant and effective over time."

3. Fostering a Culture of Innovation: Encourage a culture of innovation within your organization. Empower your team to explore new ideas, experiment with emerging technologies, and continuously seek ways to improve your services.

Example: "We have an internal innovation lab where our team can test new cybersecurity solutions and develop innovative approaches to address emerging threats. This culture of innovation keeps us at the forefront of the industry."

Conclusion

Selling cybersecurity is a dynamic and ongoing journey that requires a deep understanding of client needs, a commitment to continuous improvement, and the ability to stay proactive in the face of evolving threats. By building long-term partnerships, demonstrating ongoing value, and embracing innovation, you can position yourself as a trusted advisor and achieve sustained success in the cybersecurity market.

As you continue on this journey, remember that your role as an MSP is not just to sell solutions but to protect and empower your clients. Your expertise and dedication can make a significant difference in their security posture and overall business success.

Thank you for joining us on this exploration of the art and science of selling cybersecurity. We hope that the insights and strategies shared in this book will help you elevate your sales efforts, build stronger client relationships, and achieve lasting success.

Appendix: Resources and Tools

To support your ongoing success, we've compiled a list of useful resources, tools, and references that can help you stay informed and enhance your cybersecurity sales efforts.

Industry Reports and Publications:

- **Verizon Data Breach Investigations Report (DBIR):** Comprehensive analysis of data breach trends and insights.
- **Ponemon Institute Reports:** Research on cybersecurity trends, data breaches, and cost analyses.

Training Programs and Certifications:

- **Certified Information Systems Security Professional (CISSP):** A globally recognized certification for cybersecurity professionals.
- **Certified Ethical Hacker (CEH):** Training in ethical hacking techniques and tools.

Threat Intelligence Platforms:

- **IBM X-Force Exchange:** A threat intelligence sharing platform.
- **Recorded Future:** Real-time threat intelligence and analysis.

Professional Associations:

- **ISACA:** Information Systems Audit and Control Association, offering certifications and resources.
- **(ISC)²:** International Information System Security Certification Consortium, providing certifications and professional development.

Books and Articles:

- **"Cybersecurity and Cyberwar: What Everyone Needs to

Know" by P.W. Singer and Allan Friedman:** An accessible guide to understanding cybersecurity and cyberwarfare.

- **"The CISO Handbook" by Michael Gentile and Ronald Van Geijn:** Practical advice for Chief Information Security Officers.

We hope these resources help you continue your journey as a leading MSP in the cybersecurity industry. Thank you for your dedication to protecting businesses and making the digital world a safer place.

BONUS CHAPTER: TOP 7 THINGS AN MSP MUST KNOW TO BUILD AN EFFECTIVE CYBERSECURITY SELLING PROGRAM

Building an effective cybersecurity selling program is essential for Managed Service Providers (MSPs) who want to protect their clients and grow their business. In this bonus chapter, we'll highlight the top seven things every MSP must know to create a successful cybersecurity sales strategy.

1. Understand the Evolving Threat Landscape

To effectively sell cybersecurity solutions, MSPs must stay informed about the latest threats and trends in the cybersecurity landscape. This knowledge allows you to provide relevant and timely solutions to your clients.

Key Actions:

- **Stay Updated:** Regularly review industry reports, attend cybersecurity conferences, and participate in professional forums.
- **Threat Intelligence:** Utilize threat intelligence platforms to

monitor emerging threats and vulnerabilities.

- **Client-Specific Risks:** Understand the specific threats that different industries and businesses face, and tailor your solutions accordingly.

Example: "We continuously monitor threat intelligence feeds and industry reports to stay informed about the latest cyber threats. This allows us to provide our clients with up-to-date information and proactive measures to protect their businesses."

2. Develop a Consultative Selling Approach

Successful MSPs adopt a consultative selling approach, positioning themselves as trusted advisors rather than just vendors. This approach focuses on understanding the client's needs and providing tailored solutions that address their specific challenges.

Key Actions:

- **Ask Questions:** Engage clients in conversations to uncover their pain points, challenges, and goals.
- **Listen Actively:** Pay attention to the client's concerns and demonstrate empathy and understanding.
- **Tailored Solutions:** Develop customized cybersecurity strategies that align with the client's business objectives.

Example: "During our initial consultations, we ask detailed questions to understand our clients' specific challenges and goals. This helps us develop tailored cybersecurity strategies that address their unique needs and build strong, trusting relationships."

3. Demonstrate ROI and Financial Impact

Clients need to see the tangible value of investing in cybersecurity. By conducting financial impact analyses and demonstrating the return on investment (ROI) of your solutions, you can make a compelling case that resonates with decision-makers.

Key Actions:

- **Risk Assessment:** Identify and quantify the potential financial impact of cyber threats on the client's business.
- **Cost-Benefit Analysis:** Compare the costs of implementing cybersecurity solutions to the potential savings from avoiding breaches and disruptions.
- **Visual Aids:** Use charts, graphs, and infographics to illustrate the financial benefits.

Example: "We conduct detailed financial impact analyses to show our clients the potential savings from avoiding cyber incidents. By presenting clear ROI calculations, we help clients understand the financial benefits of investing in cybersecurity."

4. Build Trust Through Transparency

Trust is the foundation of any successful client relationship. Being transparent about your solutions, processes, and limitations helps build credibility and fosters long-term partnerships.

Key Actions:

- **Clear Communication:** Provide clients with regular updates on their security status and any actions taken.
- **Admit Mistakes:** If an error occurs, acknowledge it promptly and explain the steps being taken to resolve it.
- **Set Realistic Expectations:** Be honest about what your solutions can and cannot do, and set achievable goals.

Example: "We maintain open lines of communication with our clients, providing regular updates and transparent reports. When an issue arises, we address it immediately and keep the client informed throughout the resolution process."

5. Leverage Success Stories and Testimonials

Real-world examples of how your solutions have benefited other clients are powerful tools for building credibility and attracting new business. Success stories and testimonials provide social proof and help potential clients feel confident in choosing your services.

Key Actions:

- **Collect Testimonials:** Ask satisfied clients to share their positive experiences and specific benefits they've gained.
- **Craft Case Studies:** Develop detailed case studies that illustrate the client's journey from challenge to success.
- **Share Widely:** Use testimonials and case studies in sales presentations, on your website, and in marketing materials.

Example: "We regularly collect testimonials from satisfied clients and develop case studies that highlight our successes. These stories are featured on our website and in sales presentations, providing potential clients with tangible proof of our expertise and effectiveness."

6. Provide Comprehensive Training and Education

Educating your clients about cybersecurity is crucial for maintaining a secure environment. By offering comprehensive training and resources, you empower clients to recognize and respond to threats effectively.

Key Actions:

- **Employee Training:** Conduct regular training sessions to educate employees about common threats and best practices.
- **Resource Library:** Provide clients with access to educational materials, such as guides, articles, and videos.
- **Ongoing Support:** Offer continuous education and support to ensure clients stay updated on the latest cybersecurity practices.

Example: "We provide our clients with a comprehensive cybersecurity training program that includes regular workshops and access to a resource library. This ongoing education helps clients maintain a high level of security awareness and preparedness."

7. Foster a Culture of Continuous Improvement

The cybersecurity landscape is constantly evolving, and so should your services. Fostering a culture of continuous improvement within your organization ensures that you stay ahead of emerging threats and provide the best possible solutions to your clients.

Key Actions:

- **Continuous Learning:** Encourage your team to pursue ongoing education and certifications.
- **Innovation Lab:** Create a dedicated space for experimenting with new technologies and solutions.
- **Client Feedback:** Regularly seek feedback from clients to identify areas for improvement and innovation.

Example: "We have established an internal innovation lab where our team can test new cybersecurity technologies and develop innovative solutions. This commitment to continuous improvement allows us to stay ahead of emerging threats and offer cutting-edge services to our clients."

Conclusion

Building an effective cybersecurity selling program requires a deep understanding of the threat landscape, a consultative selling approach, and a commitment to transparency, education, and continuous improvement. By focusing on these key areas, MSPs can differentiate themselves from the competition, build strong client relationships, and achieve lasting success in the cybersecurity market.

Thank you for joining us on this journey through the art and science of selling cybersecurity. We hope that the insights and strategies shared in this book will help you elevate your sales efforts, protect your clients, and build a successful, rewarding career as an MSP.

BONUS CHAPTER: THREATCAPTAIN - COMPREHENSIVE SAAS SOLUTION FOR MSPS

Product Overview

ThreatCaptain is an all-in-one SaaS platform designed to empower Managed Service Providers (MSPs) with the tools and insights needed to build an effective cybersecurity selling program. By addressing the top seven critical aspects of cybersecurity sales, ThreatCaptain enables MSPs to stay ahead of emerging threats, engage clients consultatively, demonstrate ROI, build trust, leverage success stories, provide comprehensive training, and foster continuous improvement.

Product and Feature List

1. **Threat Intelligence and Monitoring**
   - **Real-Time Threat Updates:** Continuous updates on the latest cyber threats and vulnerabilities.
   - **Threat Analysis Dashboard:** Centralized dashboard displaying current threat landscape, customized for each client's industry and size.
   - **Automated Alerts:** Instant notifications of new threats

relevant to the MSP's clients.

2. **Consultative Sales Tools**
- **Client Assessment Module:** Tools to conduct detailed assessments of clients' cybersecurity posture.
- **Needs Analysis Templates:** Pre-built templates for identifying client pain points and goals.
- **Customizable Solution Builder:** Create tailored cybersecurity solutions based on client-specific needs.

3. **Financial Impact and ROI Analysis**
- **Risk Quantification Engine:** Converts cyber risks into financial terms, highlighting potential losses from breaches.
- **Cost-Benefit Analysis Tools:** Compare the costs of cybersecurity investments with potential savings.
- **ROI Calculator:** Demonstrate the return on investment of proposed cybersecurity measures.

4. **Transparency and Reporting**
- **Comprehensive Reporting Suite:** Generate detailed reports on client cybersecurity posture, risk assessments, and action plans.
- **Client Portal:** Secure, accessible portal for clients to view their cybersecurity status, reports, and recommendations.
- **Automated Report Generation:** Schedule and automate regular report delivery to clients.

5. **Success Stories and Testimonials**
- **Case Study Builder:** Create detailed case studies showcasing successful client outcomes.
- **Testimonial Collection Tool:** Easily gather and manage client testimonials.

- **Marketing Integration:** Integrate success stories and testimonials into sales presentations and marketing materials.

6. **Training and Education**
- **Training Modules:** Comprehensive cybersecurity training programs for client employees.
- **Resource Library:** Access to a wide range of educational materials, including guides, articles, and videos.
- **Interactive Workshops:** Virtual and in-person workshops to train clients on the latest cybersecurity practices.

7. **Continuous Improvement Tools**
- **Ongoing Learning Hub:** Access to the latest research, trends, and best practices in cybersecurity.
- **Innovation Lab:** A sandbox environment for testing new cybersecurity technologies and solutions.
- **Feedback Loop:** Collect and analyze client feedback to continuously improve services and solutions.

Additional Features
- **Compliance Management:** Tools to help clients meet industry-specific compliance requirements (e.g., GDPR, HIPAA).
- **Integration Capabilities:** Seamless integration with existing MSP tools and client systems.
- **User-Friendly Interface:** Intuitive interface designed for ease of use by both MSPs and clients.
- **Scalability:** Scalable solutions to accommodate businesses of all sizes and growth stages.
- **Customer Support:** Dedicated support team available 24/7 to assist with any issues or questions.

BONUS CHAPTER: USING FINANCIAL IMPACT SIMULATIONS TO ENHANCE CYBERSECURITY SALES

Introduction

In the rapidly evolving world of cybersecurity, Managed Service Providers (MSPs) must be equipped with tools that not only highlight the importance of robust security measures but also quantify their financial impact. ThreatCaptain is the revolutionary SaaS platform designed specifically for MSPs to help them demonstrate the financial consequences of cyber threats to their clients. This chapter will explore how to use financial impact simulations to show clients how their cybersecurity posture —comprising security controls, risk mitigation documents, compliance and insurance, security policies, leadership, and training—affects the likelihood and impact of cyber breaches.

The Need for Financial Impact Simulations

One of the biggest challenges MSPs face is convincing clients of the tangible benefits of investing in cybersecurity. Many businesses, especially small to mid-sized enterprises (SMEs), often view cybersecurity as a cost rather than an investment. Financial impact simulations help bridge this gap by translating cybersecurity risks into financial terms that clients can easily understand.

Key Benefits:

- **Quantifies Risks:** Converts complex cybersecurity threats into clear financial impacts.
- **Justifies Investments:** Demonstrates the ROI of cybersecurity measures.
- **Enhances Decision-Making:** Provides data-driven insights for strategic decisions.
- **Builds Trust:** Positions the MSP as a strategic advisor using advanced analytics.

Introducing ThreatCaptain

ThreatCaptain is a cybersecurity sales enablement platform that empowers MSPs by providing realistic simulations and financial impact analyses. It helps MSPs quantify cyber risks and present them in a way that is understandable and compelling for clients.

Key Features:

- **Realistic Simulations:** Uses behavior patterns from known threats to assess likelihood and impact.
- **Industry-Driven Insights:** Translates cybersecurity risks into financial terms.
- **Strategic Reporting:** Generates executive-friendly reports for effective decision-making.
- **Proactive Risk Management:** Enables continuous monitoring and threat simulation.

Example from ThreatCaptain Whitepaper: "ThreatCaptain's RedPill platform conducts an initial analysis of a potential client's cyber risk profile, providing a detailed report that quantifies the financial impact of potential cyber threats, which serves as a clear baseline for discussion".

Conducting Financial Impact Simulations

Here's how to use ThreatCaptain to conduct financial impact simulations and enhance your cybersecurity sales efforts:

1. Initial Consultation and Risk Analysis: Begin by conducting an initial risk analysis using ThreatCaptain's RedPill platform. This involves assessing the client's current cybersecurity posture, including their security controls, risk mitigation documents, compliance and insurance policies, security policies, leadership, and training programs.

Key Actions:

- **Assess Current Posture:** Evaluate the client's existing cybersecurity measures and identify potential vulnerabilities.
- **Simulate Threats:** Use ThreatCaptain to simulate realistic cyber threats based on the client's industry and size.
- **Generate Report:** Produce a detailed report that quantifies the financial impact of potential cyber threats.

Example: "During an initial consultation with a healthcare provider, we used ThreatCaptain to simulate potential ransomware attacks. The platform generated a report showing the financial impact of a successful attack, highlighting the cost of recovery, legal fees, and reputational damage".

2. Quarterly Business Reviews (QBRs): For existing clients, integrate ThreatCaptain into your Quarterly Business Reviews. Regularly update the risk analysis to reflect any changes in the client's business operations or the threat landscape.

Key Actions:

- **Update Risk Profile:** Reassess the client's cybersecurity posture and update the threat simulations.
- **Present Findings:** Share updated reports with the client during QBRs, highlighting any changes in risk levels and the

financial implications.

- **Recommend Adjustments:** Provide tailored recommendations for improving the client's cybersecurity posture based on the latest analysis.

Example: "During a QBR with a retail client, we presented an updated risk analysis report that showed an increase in phishing attacks. Using ThreatCaptain's data, we recommended additional employee training and enhanced email security measures".

3. Tailored Cybersecurity Recommendations: Utilize the insights gained from ThreatCaptain to provide targeted cybersecurity recommendations. These should be customized to address the specific risks and financial implications identified in the simulations.

Key Actions:

- **Identify Key Risks:** Highlight the most significant threats based on the financial impact analysis.
- **Recommend Solutions:** Suggest specific cybersecurity measures, such as advanced threat detection systems, updated security policies, or additional training.
- **Create a Roadmap:** Develop a strategic plan for implementing the recommended measures over time.

Example: "Based on the financial impact analysis for a financial services firm, we recommended implementing multi-factor authentication and conducting regular vulnerability assessments. These measures were prioritized in a strategic roadmap that aligned with the client's budget and business goals".

4. Justification for Cybersecurity Investments: Use the financial data generated by ThreatCaptain to build a compelling case for proposed cybersecurity investments. Show how the cost of preventive measures compares to the potential financial losses from a breach.

Key Actions:

- **Compare Costs and Benefits:** Present a cost-benefit analysis that highlights the ROI of cybersecurity investments.
- **Highlight Savings:** Emphasize the potential savings from avoiding breaches, including direct costs (e.g., recovery, legal fees) and indirect costs (e.g., reputational damage, operational disruptions).
- **Visualize Data:** Use charts and graphs to make the financial data easily understandable.

Example: "We used ThreatCaptain to show a logistics company that the cost of implementing advanced threat detection was significantly lower than the potential financial impact of a data breach. This clear financial justification helped secure approval for the investment".

5. Preparation for Cyber Insurance Applications: ThreatCaptain's methodology aligns with the assessment criteria used by cyber insurance providers. Use the platform to prepare clients for the insurance application process, potentially qualifying them for better terms.

Key Actions:

- **Assess Compliance:** Ensure the client's cybersecurity measures meet the requirements of cyber insurance providers.
- **Generate Reports:** Provide detailed risk assessment reports that can be included in the insurance application.
- **Recommend Improvements:** Suggest any additional measures needed to enhance the client's cybersecurity posture and improve insurance terms.

Example: "By using ThreatCaptain's comprehensive risk assessment, we helped a manufacturing client prepare for their cyber insurance application. The detailed report demonstrated their robust cybersecurity measures, resulting in more favorable insurance terms".

Conclusion

Using financial impact simulations through ThreatCaptain empowers MSPs to demonstrate the tangible value of cybersecurity investments. By translating complex cybersecurity risks into clear financial terms, you can make compelling cases for proactive measures, build stronger client relationships, and position yourself as a strategic advisor.

By integrating ThreatCaptain into your pre-sales consultations, quarterly business reviews, and ongoing client engagements, you transform the conversation around cybersecurity from a technical necessity to a strategic financial decision. This approach not only enhances your value proposition but also empowers your clients to make informed investments in their cybersecurity infrastructure, based on a clear understanding of the financial risks and benefits.

Printed in Great Britain
by Amazon